Worth Protecting
Women, Men, and Freedom
From Sexual Aggression

By Pamela Woll and Terence T. Gorski

For Margaret —

Best wishes in bring
dignity & healing
into people's lives.

— P. Woll

Additional copies are available from the publisher:
  Herald House/ Independence Press
  3225 South Noland Road
  P.O. Box 1770
  Independence, MO 64055-0770
  Phone: 1-800-767-8181 or 816/252-5010

Excerpts from *I Never Called It Rape: The Ms. Report on Recognizing, Fighting, and Surviving Date Rape* by Robin Warshaw (HarperCollins, 1988) are used with permission of HarperCollins Publishers.

Library of Congress Cataloging-in-Publication Data
Gorski, Terence T.
   Worth protecting : women, men, and freedom from sexual aggression /
   Terence T. Gorski, Pamela Woll.
        p.   cm.
   Includes bibliographical references.
   ISBN 0-8309-0702-5
   1. Sex crimes—United States.   2. Sex crimes—Prevention—United States. 3. Man–Woman relationships—United States.
I. Woll, Pamela, 1952–   . II. Title.
HV6592.G67   1995   95-8001
364.1'53 0973—dc20   CIP
Item No. 17-026059

99 98 97 96 95   1 2 3 4 5

If getting someone to bed against their will becomes one's mission, he may succeed with their body, but in the process he will waste their soul. He will not feel that exchange of spirits after which one walks away having gathered life. He will sense a small death because he has fastened himself onto a cadaver.

—Hugh Prather
Notes on Love and Courage

Contents

Acknowledgments 11
Foreword by Terence T. Gorski 13

Part I: Where We Are 17

Chapter 1: Worth Protecting 19
    Two Sides 20
    No Simple Formula 22
    About This Book 25
    Sexual Force and Manipulation 26
    Choices and Choice Points 28
    Responsibility 29
    Who's Worth Protecting? 32

Part II: What We Find 35

Chapter 2: A Losing Battle 37
    Why Haven't Things Changed? 38
    Effects of the Old Model 38
        Don 39
        Sandy 42
        What Happens Next? 44
    Effects of the New Model 46
Chapter 3: The Old Model of Relationship 51
    Phase One: Humiliation 53
    Phase Two: Fear-Based Beliefs 54
    Phase Three: Broken Thinking 57
    Phase Four: Panic and Power Games 59
    Phase Five: Victimization 62
    Jumping Models 63
        Transformation 64
        Being Honest About Payoffs 65
        Hope 66
Chapter 4: The New Model of Relationship 69

Phase One: Dignity 71
Phase Two: Beliefs Based on Love 72
Phase Three: Whole Thinking 75
Phase Four: Friendship 77
Phase Five: Respect 79

Part III: How We Got Here 83

Chapter 5: Our Legacy 85
Evolution and the Brain 86
   The Deeper Brain 87
   The Higher Brain 87
   The Whole Brain 88
   Brain Chemicals 89
   Do We Have Any Choice? 90
The Evolution of Gender Roles 90
   The Beginning of Commodity Thinking 91
The Growth of Civilizations 93
   Myths About Women's Sexuality 94
   Myths About Men's Roles 95
   Old and New Messages 96
Building a Different Future 97
Chapter 6: The Commodity Culture 99
Women as Commodities 100
   The Economics of Being Female 102
Men as Commodities 104
   The Economics of Being Male 107
Real Women, Real Men, Real Friendship 108
Real Power, True Worth 110
Chapter 7: Growing Up 113
Self-Esteem: Self-Worth, Self-Confidence,
   and Self-Respect 115
   How Children Learn the Skills of Self-Esteem 116
   Self-Esteem and Sexual Aggression 117
   Strengthening Self-Esteem Skills 118
Learning About Gender and Relationship Roles . . . 120

Becoming Individuals 120
Becoming Women and Men 122
Relating to the Opposite Sex 123
The Need to Resolve 125
Boundaries 126
The Two Extremes 126
Boundaries in Women's Lives 127
Boundaries in Men's Lives 129
The Effects of Trauma and Abuse 131
What Makes It Trauma? 132
Childhood Abuse and Sexual Aggression 133
"It Was My Fault" 134
Denial 135
Resiliency—Strength and Flexibility 136
Getting Help for Childhood Wounds 138

Part IV: Sexual Involvement 141

Chapter 8: Communication in Sexual Involvement 143
Communication in the Old and New Models 143
Sexual Limits 144
Verbal and Nonverbal Communication 145
New-Model Communication 146
Communication Based on Self-Knowledge 146
Clear and Direct Communication 147
Respect for Ourselves and Others 149
Assertive Messages 152
Staying Appropriate for the Situation 154
Staying Clean and Sober 158
Awkwardness in Healthy Communication 159
Chapter 9: The Stages of Sexual Involvement 163
Mapping the Stages 163
Movement from Stage to Stage 165
Honesty 166
Dignity and Well-Being 167
Your Effect on the Relationship 167

Stage One: Acknowledgment of Attraction 168
  Acknowledgment of Attraction in the New Model . . 168
  Acknowledgment of Attraction in the Old Model . . . 170
  Safety Measures in Acknowledgment of Attraction . . 171
Stage Two: Flirting 172
  Flirting in the New Model 173
  Flirting in the Old Model 174
  Safety Measures in the Flirting Stage 177
Stage Three: Sensual Involvement 179
  Sensual Involvement in the New Model 180
  Sensual Involvement in the Old Model 181
  Safety Measures in Sensual Involvement 183
Stage Four: Sexual Involvement 185
  Sexual Involvement in the New Model 185
  Sexual Involvement in the Old Model 186
  Safety Measures in Sexual Involvement 186
Healthy Sexuality in the New Model 188

Part V: Sexual Force and Manipulation 191

Chapter 10: The Continuum of Sexual Aggression 193
The Continuum of Aggression 194
Sexual Assertiveness 195
Seduction 197
  When Men are Seduced 199
  Breaking the Power of Seduction 201
Psychological Force 202
  Resisting Psychological Force 204
  Common Excuses for Using Psychological Force . . 205
Threat of Physical Force 206
  Giving in to the Threat 207
Physical Force 208
  Why Don't Some Women Fight Back? 210
  Men Who Don't Know It's Rape 212
  Breaking the Pattern 215
Systematic Desensitization—Playing the Continuum . 216

The Skill of the Manipulator 218
Getting Help 219
Why Do Some Men Become Aggressive? 220
Help for Sexually Aggressive Men 222
Women Who Want to Help 223
Chapter 11: The Effects of Sexual Aggression 227
Effects on the Victims 229
 • Seduction 229
 • Psychological Force 230
 • Threat of Physical Force 231
 • Physical Force 232
Effects on People Who Use Sexual Force 236
 • Seduction 236
 • Psychological Force 237
 • Threat of Physical Force 238
 • Physical Force 239

Part VI: Hope and Healing 241

Chapter 12: The Healing Process 243
Letting Others In 244
Skills That Reduce Fear and Danger 246
The Feelings of Grief 248
 Denial 249
 Self-Blame 250
 Depression 251
 Isolation 253
 Anger 254
 Acceptance 256
Broken Dreams, Transformation, and Hope 257
Chapter 13: Chemical Dependency, Recovery,
 and Sexual Aggression 261
Medicating the Pain—Causing More Pain 262
Powerlessness vs. Helplessness 264
The Urge to Escape 265
 Escaping Into Relationships 266

9

The "Thirteenth Step" 268
    Thirteenth Stepping by Helping Professionals 270
    Safety from the Thirteenth Step 271
    Waiting for Sober Relationships 272
Chapter 14: Safety and Friendship 277
    Going Slowly 278
    The Stages and Levels of Relationship 279
    Friendship 281
Afterword to Therapists 285
Bibliography 289

Tables and Diagrams

Old and New Models of Relationship 24
Old Model of Relationship 52
Fear-Based Beliefs 56
Broken Thinking 58
Panic and Power Games 61
New Model of Relationship 68
Beliefs Based on Love 74
Whole Thinking 76
Friendship 79
Four Stages of Sexual Involvement 164
Safety in Acknowledgment 171
Safety in Flirting 175
Safety Tips for Women on the First Few Dates 176
Safety in Sensual Involvement 184
Safety in Sexual Involvement 187
Continuum of Sexual Aggression 194
Some Warning Signs of Rape 209
What to Do if You're Confronted with Rape 214
Signs of Systematic Desensitization 217

Acknowledgments

First of all, both of us thank the many people who have told their stories of pain, fear, and frustration—and of hope, healing, and true freedom. These stories have been collected over many years, through Terry's clinical practice and speaking and writing career, Pam's years as a writer, and both authors' research for this book. Some of these stories are retold in this book, with enough details changed to protect the privacy of the people who lived them. But many more have joined the general mix of information, to help broaden and deepen our understanding of this difficult subject.

Although *Worth Protecting* is truly the collaborative effort of its authors, many other people have provided professional support, suggestions, information, and insight. Their input has added texture and depth. Deep appreciation goes to William L. White, M.A., of Lighthouse Institute for his generous and thoughtful input and support throughout the planning, writing, and review process.

Gratitude also goes to the following people, who have given their professional feedback and, in many cases, reviewed drafts of the book: Fernando Ares, M.A., Illinois Alcohol and Drug Dependence Association; Claudia Black, Ph.D.; Bob Carty, M.S.W., CADC, Grant Hospital; Denise Eaves, LSCW, CEAP, Loyola University Chicago; Maya Hennessey, CRADC, Illinois Department of Alcoholism and Substance Abuse; Robert Kearney, Ph.D., Robert Kearney and Associates; Paul Kivel, Oakland Men's Project; John Knaus, M.D.; Andra Medea, M.A., Medea and Associates; Gingi Napoli, Public Allies; Grace Jo O'Leary, addictions counselor; Hugh and Gayle Prather; Glenn Richardson, CSADC, Illinois Alcohol and Other Drug Abuse Professional Certification Association; Chris Scott, Ph.D, Lighthouse Institute; Joseph Troiani, Ph.D., Will County Department of Mental Health; and Marie Tyse, chief of police, University of Illinois at Chicago.

Additional thanks go to others who have reviewed drafts of the book, including Barbara Allen, Rick Dillner, Rory Guerra, Steven Guerra, Valerie Jefferson, Tom Johnson, Kathy Larsson, Howard Mandel, Debbie Rafine, Ann Richards, Gerald Rawling, Gillan Rawling, Michael Smith, Marion O'Malley Woll, and John Wood.

Pam also extends special thanks to three groups of people: To the Prevention Resource Center (PRC) and its parent corporation, Prevention First, thanks for the flexibility that has made it possible for her to work on this book outside her role as senior writer for PRC. Their vision and commitment to quality have given her the best possible preparation for her contribution to *Worth Protecting*. To the faculty at DePaul University's School for New Learning, thanks for the guidance and support of this project; and special gratitude to Jean Knoll, Ph.D., for being the best faculty mentor imaginable. And to her family, deepest love and thanks for being wonderful and teaching her how to love.

And finally, both authors extend love and gratitude to Carmela Liotta, C.A.C., founder of A New Pathway, for her love, friendship, support, and amazing enthusiasm throughout the writing process.

Pam Woll and Terry Gorski

Foreword

Books come together in all kinds of ways. This is especially true of collaborative works. *Worth Protecting* came together peacefully and naturally, as if it were sitting there all along waiting to be written. Pam Woll and I were just the right people to write it.

I had been wanting to work on this topic for quite a while. In my twenty-five years as a counselor and therapist, I had seen time and time again the pain that my clients of both genders experienced in sexual and romantic relationships. In my work in chemical dependency and relapse prevention, I saw the large part this pain played in so many people's relapse patterns.

That realization led me to write *Getting Love Right: Learning the Choices of Healthy Intimacy*, and to develop a series of lectures and workshop presentations on the topic, along with a PBS special. And as I toured the country talking and listening to men and women, I kept hearing strong emotions and hard questions about date rape and other kinds of abuse in relationships.

At one lecture I was talking about techniques women could use to protect themselves from the possibility of date rape, and three women stood up and challenged me. "You shouldn't teach women to prevent rape," they said. "Rape is the man's responsibility. You should be talking to men about this."

Then another group of women stood up and said, "Wait a minute, we want to hear it. We're going to be out there in dating situations with nobody there to protect us. We want to know how to protect ourselves." So I finished my presentation. It would have been nice if all men who had sexual aggression problems were there that night deciding never to rape again, but I couldn't count on it. Those women couldn't count on it, either.

My work with criminal offenders and victims of crime led me further into my questions about abuse and sexual aggression in relationships. How can some men do these things to women? How can some women let them? How can some men rape women and have no idea that that's what they're doing? What does all this say about us as men and women?

It was about that time that I first mentioned the idea to Pam Woll, a talented writer, researcher, and speaker whose work I had admired in the years I had known her. Pam's research and writing on a wide range of topics, from violence prevention to spirituality, gave her the open mind and broad perspective this topic needed. Pam sent me a proposal, and I called to tell her I was very interested in working with her on this book.

As we spoke, it became clear that our collaboration wouldn't be just a woman defending women's positions and a man defending men's positions. It would be two people with different experiences, each caring as much about the well-being of the other gender as we did about our own. Neither one of us wanted to see the rights of one sex "win out" over the rights of the other. We knew that, if that happened, nobody would win.

When Pam and I began the research and long phone conversations that led to *Worth Protecting*, we soon realized that we couldn't just look at the extreme cases of abuse and aggression. Those extremes are the logical extensions of intricate social arrangements between women and men in general. Our whole social system teaches each gender to think of members of the opposite sex as commodities. The problem of sexual aggression is a systemwide problem that entraps individuals and leads them to make poor decisions.

In tackling this problem we couldn't just look at rape and other sexual aggression. We also had to look at the more subtle forms of manipulation in relationships. These sometimes lead to rape and abuse, but more often they just destroy the trust and friendship. We couldn't limit our vision to the ways men use and manipulate women, either. We had to take an honest look at the ways in which men are used and manipulated. And we couldn't just look at deliberate, premeditated rape. We also had to look at how men and women fail to communicate their desires and limits.

Pam and I quickly understood that, as different as our experiences were, we agreed on some important concepts. Any solution to the problem of sexual aggression and manipulation has to involve the acceptance of mutual responsibility between women and men. We must all work together to create a climate of friendship and mutual value intead of competition and commodity thinking. Without those things, we're setting ourselves up for manipulation and aggression.

As *Worth Protecting* developed, both Pam and I found these convictions growing in our individual lives and relationships. In our collaborative process we worked through our disagreements, grew through our solutions, learned throughout our discoveries, and thoroughly enjoyed the development of a book that neither of us could have written on our own.

Freedom from sexual aggression and manipulation is not just an escape from pain and danger. It is the discovery that love and desire are not the opposite of friendship and respect. It is the discovery of the men and women we were born to be. We also have a lot to gain from this journey of discovery, and a lot to lose if we stay where we've been all along. As you read *Worth Protecting* we hope you will join us on this journey.

Terence T. Gorski

PART I

Where
We Are

CHAPTER 1

Worth Protecting

It's a typical night.

Julie double-latches the door when Ed leaves. She didn't want to have sex with him, but somehow she was talked into it. In a way, she felt as if she owed it to him. After all, he took her out for dinner and drinks, and spent time listening to her troubles. Maybe she thought it would take away some of her lonely, empty feelings. It didn't.

Across town, Brad is driving Sarah home in silence. It's their first date, and in the restaurant Sarah told him she'd been warned about date rape. With a stern look on her face, she outlined a set of rules that he'd have to follow if they were going to spend time together. He left the restaurant feeling confused, misunderstood, and insulted. He still feels that way, but he's too proud to say it.

Walking in the woods, Lisa feels a little alarmed when John's arm drops lower and lower on her back, but she says nothing. She finds it hard to believe that a well-respected young man like John would try anything. Later tonight he'll rape her, brutally, on a bed of dry leaves and twigs.

As Peggy says "No" and pushes Ron back against the steering wheel, several voices are going off in his head. One is laughing: "It's a game. She wants it!" Another, speaking calmly, says "Give her time. You like her." A third voice is screaming, "It's too late! I can't stop!" And underneath them all, his father's voice is yelling: "Fight back, you little sissy! Be a man!"

Larry is thinking about his walk with Beth earlier this evening. She said a lot of things that made it clear she was interested. Then later, when they were walking, she got kind of quiet when he put his arm around her and kissed her. He wondered if she might really be more shy than he'd ever imagined. She's interested, though. He can tell.

Beth is on the phone with a friend, describing the way Larry kept putting his arm around her while they walked and the inappropriately sexual way he kissed her. She felt scared and violated. It brought back a lot of bad feelings from sexual abuse in her childhood. But it never occurred to her to push him away or tell him to stop. Now she's furious. "I feel like I've been raped!" she tells her friend.

In the next apartment, Dawn stands in the shower and lets the hot water mix with her tears and turn her body red. She remembers the way his arms felt, pinning her shoulders and pulling off her clothes, and the way his legs pushed her knees apart. She doesn't understand it. Jack had acted like a friend until that moment. She struggled and yelled "No," but he forced her to have sex anyway. Now she feels like a tramp. It hasn't occurred to her yet that she's just been raped.

Two Sides

Of course, these aren't the only kinds of pictures that make up this night. At the other end of the scale there are people who are laughing and happy and peaceful—people who are safe with friends who care. There are people whose sexuality is a gift that they give to one another—if and when they're both ready. It's given with affection and respect, expecting nothing but the same in return.

But for others, their sexuality is being used tonight. It has become a weapon of war, a prize to be won, a city to be stormed, the price of survival, evidence of manhood, bait for a trap, payment for attention or drugs—even a desperate cry for help. And there are those whose sexual safety will be sacrificed just because they lack the knowledge and skill to protect it.

All our lives we've been taught about the age-old "battle of the sexes." We've seen so much conflict around us that we can't help believing in that battle. Now we hear about the sexual manipulation that leaves both genders feeling used and betrayed; the rise in date rape in high school, college, and beyond; the women whose emotional health is destroyed by those experiences; the men who feel they have no choice but to use force to get sex; and the men who are falsely accused of rape and suffer ruined reputations.[1]

> **Some people's sexual safety is sacrificed just because they lack the knowledge and skill to protect it.**

Are men and women really natural enemies? Are men all-powerful, abusing their power out of anger and an urge to dominate? Are women sly and tricky, luring men in and then saying no just to humiliate them? Are women and men from different species, designed to use and mistrust one another?

The authors of this book would answer "no" to all those questions. There are some men who really want to hurt and use women, and some women who really want to hurt and use men. But most of us—of both genders—are just confused. We haven't even been taught how to understand or communicate well with ourselves—much less with one another.

Women and men are more alike than we might ever imagine. People of both genders often feel used, betrayed, suspi-

21

cious, awkward, angry, confused, and misunderstood by the opposite sex. And in many cases, when people really are victimized, the "victim" and the "victimizer" both feel humiliated, powerless, and worthless at heart. We've been taught different ways of reacting to our pain and fear, but pain is pain, and fear is fear.

This book is for anyone, male or female, who wants to understand and rise above the current epidemic of sexual force and manipulation.

> **"Victims" and "victimizers" both feel humiliated, powerless, and worthless at heart.**

No Simple Formula

If only these problems were simple! If only we could come up with a formula that fits all the ways people are forced, seduced, scared, or tricked into having sex with people they've known and trusted.

Maybe then we could understand the problems of sexual force and manipulation. We could protect all the people who would otherwise be raped in new or old relationships. We could save the frustration and betrayal people feel when they're talked or tricked into having sex. We could protect all the friendships that will otherwise die before they have a chance to be born.

Worth Protecting doesn't offer a simple formula for understanding or preventing sexual aggression and manipulation. Instead it offers a framework that's large enough to include the many forces that lead to these problems. It shows, wherever possible, how these forces fit together and feed off one another. And it offers a vision of respectful friendship and safety between women and men—and the skills to help turn that vision into reality.

The framework that holds both the problem and the vision is a set of two models of relationship—the old and new models. The old, destructive model of relationship is a "vicious circle" that starts and ends with humiliation for both partners. In this model the partners tend to take different roles, but both end up losing. It robs us of the very things it promises to give us; things like intimacy, strength, confidence, self-worth, self-respect, and peace of mind. The old model comes from our history as men and women, the messages we hear from the popular culture, and our life experiences—particularly in childhood.

The new model of relationship is also a circle, but it begins and ends with dignity. In the new model we might get hurt—because getting hurt is a part of life—but we won't be as likely to be used, betrayed, or attacked by people we trust. And we won't feel the need to use, betray, or attack others. The good news is that it's possible to jump from the old to the new model.

The new model has room for passion. It has room for erotic thoughts, dreams, and desires. But in this model we don't try to separate people's sexuality from their humanity. We know that these things can't be separated, and that our efforts to separate them would only damage both partners.

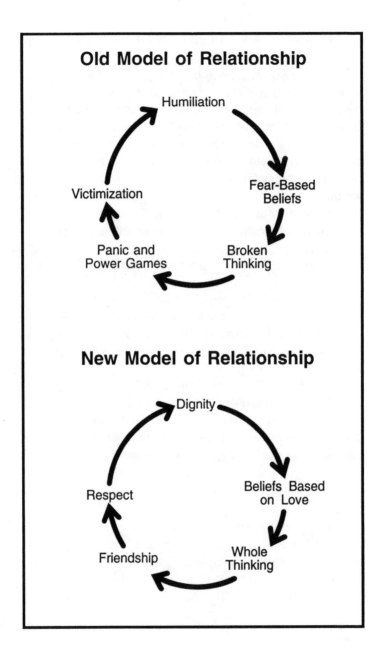

Old Model of Relationship

Humiliation

Fear-Based Beliefs

Broken Thinking

Panic and Power Games

Victimization

New Model of Relationship

Dignity

Beliefs Based on Love

Whole Thinking

Friendship

Respect

About This Book

Worth Protecting is for men and women, from their early teens through their adult years. It is meant to build hope and dignity where we often find confusion, humiliation, and anger. The chapters that follow are organized in five parts:

Part II: The old model of relationship that's kept the "battle of the sexes" alive and the new model that can bring us to respect and friendship

Part III: How our history, cultures, and childhood experiences often lead to sexual force and manipulation

Part IV: The stages of sexual involvement, and how we communicate—or fail to communicate—about our sexual desires and limits

Part V: The scale or "continuum" of sexual aggression—from sexual assertiveness to rape—and the effects of each point on that scale

Part VI: Hope for healing the wounds of sexual force and living lives of respect, friendship, and safety

Each chapter ends with a set of "Journal Questions" that can be used for discussion or as topics for an ongoing journal. The book can be used alone, or with the *Worth Protecting* workbook. The workbook has exercises that individuals and groups can use to build understanding and skills.

Worth Protecting was written by a woman and a man together for good reasons. We've needed a guidebook on this subject that would speak to both sexes. Much of the conflict between us comes from the fact that we've been taking our cues from separate scripts. This book is designed to teach specific skills and choices, and to help each gender understand what the other is going through.

Most of the skills and models in this book will be useful to people of any sexual orientation—gay, lesbian, or "straight" (heterosexual). But many of the problems described here will be much more common in straight relationships. That's because these problems are rooted in the roles men and women have been trained to take on in relationships with one another.

Sexual Force and Manipulation

The first obstacle we run into when we try to deal with the problem of sexual aggression is that we don't have a clear and common language for it. How can we sort these ideas out in our own minds, much less talk to one another about them? The many kinds of aggression are laid out in detail in chapter ten. Meanwhile, here's a quick look at how the terms "sexual force," "rape," "date rape," and "sexual manipulation" will be used in this book.

Sexual force is used to mean anything sexual that's done by physical or psychological force, against someone's wishes. That includes touching someone sexually against his or her will. It also might include other ways of invading someone's sexual privacy. Rape is also an act of sexual force, and some kinds of sexual manipulation are done with the use of psychological force.

Rape is sex that takes place against someone's wishes. It's entry into someone's vagina, mouth, or anus that's done without that person's consent—by physical force or the threat of physical force. Rape can be committed by one person or by several people. The object most often used for entry is a man's penis, but sometimes other objects are used. The amount of force can be just enough for penetration, or the rape can be accompanied by other violence, up to and including murder.

26

This book is concerned with rape that happens between people who are in relationships, or getting to know one another and exploring the possibility of relationships. In some cases this is called "date rape," although the traditional "date" is no longer the only setting in which we can get to know people we might be interested in—socially, romantically, or sexually.

Sexual Force and Manipulation

Sexual Force: Sexual acts done by physical or psychological force, against someone's wishes.

Rape: Sex against someone's wishes, by physical force or the threat of physical force.

Sexual Manipulation: The use of dishonest or indirect tactics to get sex, or the use of sexual attraction to get other things.

Rape can take place even if both partners are strongly attracted to one another, and even if they've had sex before. It's the fact that one partner is forced or threatened that makes it rape.

For simplicity's sake, *Worth Protecting* often describes rape as being done to a woman by a man. Of course, this isn't always the case. Many men are raped, but in almost all cases it's by other men. And because rape doesn't always come in the form of penis/vaginal intercourse, women can also rape men or other women. But this is rare: women's social training usually doesn't lead them to rape others.

In **manipulation** we use sneaky or indirect ways of getting people to do what we want. We might use guilt, play on their sympathy, lie to them, flatter them, scare them, seduce them, try to stop them from thinking, or use a number of other tactics. **Sexual manipulation** takes on many forms. Two levels of manipulation discussed in this book are seduction and the threat of psychological force. Manipulation might be used to get sex, or sexual attraction might be used to get other things. It's important to understand all kinds of sexual manipulation, and how they fit together. It's also important to know where manipulation ends and aggression begins.

Both rape and manipulation can take place at any point in a relationship: on the night we meet, on the third date, after we've been sexually involved for months, after years of marriage, or after the relationship is over.

Choices and Choice Points

An important step in preventing sexual force and manipulation is to understand the role of choice in all this. There are some cases in which we might have little or no choice. Both men and women have been tricked by skillful manipulators. And people have been raped in situations where nothing they could have done would have prevented it.

But there are many more cases in which we do have choices, although we're not always aware of them. We're often led to think of sexual force and manipulation as single events that just happen "out of nowhere." But in social situations, these things tend to come at the end of a long line of beliefs, thoughts, feelings, words, looks, gestures, and actions. Each person involved makes decisions all along that line. We can think of those decisions as "choice points."

For example, when one person decides to ask for a date, it's a choice point. When the other says yes or no to the date, that's another choice point. When we decide where to go, what to do, how to get there, where to meet, those are all choice points. Each time we do any of the things we've decided to do—get in a car, order a drink, sit down on the couch, make a sexual move— it's a choice point for one or both partners. Even if we've made plans, we still choose whether or not to follow those plans. And each time we decide to communicate what we want or don't want—or decide how to communicate those things—it's a choice point.

Choice points are important because they show us where our freedom is. If we don't believe we have choices, it's as if we have no choices. We believe we're helpless. If a woman doesn't believe she has the right to say no, walk away, or fight back, how will she ever protect herself from manipulation and rape? If a man believes his self-worth and his manhood depend on his ability to have sex with this woman—right now—how will he ever understand that he has the power to stop himself? Our most valuable choice points may be the ones where we decide to question our beliefs about ourselves.

Choice points are important because they show us where our freedom is. If we don't believe we have choices, it's as if we have no choices.

An important choice point came when you decided to pick up this book. If you haven't been sure what your choices were in developing relationships—or if you've felt like you had no choices at all—now you've taken a step toward giving yourself more options. You've taken a step toward greater freedom.

Responsibility

Of course, if we have choices, then we also have responsibility for our actions. Many of us don't like that idea because

29

we get the word "responsibility" mixed up with the word "blame." Blame brings up images of evil, worthlessness, punishment, and being "bad people." Often these are the same kinds of images that messed up our beliefs about ourselves in the first place.

The word "responsibility" is different, though. It just means that our "stuff"—good and bad—is ours. Our beliefs, our thoughts, our feelings, our actions, and our words are *ours*. We're responsible for what we do—or don't do—and for the effects of what we do. But we're not responsible for what anybody else does, no matter what we might have done or left undone.

For example, if a single woman has heard about date rape, she has a responsibility to learn about it. She's responsible for learning what she can do to make herself less vulnerable, and doing it to the best of her ability. She's responsible for setting clear limits and sending clear and honest messages to the people she dates. But if someone rapes her, she's not responsible for having been raped—and she's certainly not to blame for it. She can't be responsible for another person's actions. It doesn't work that way.

If we've been hurt or abused—as adults or as children—there's a strong human tendency to blame ourselves. We don't realize it, but we actually decide to believe that we deserved to be hurt. It helps us pretend that what happened made sense, that it was fair, and that we have control over what happens to us. Sometimes the people who hurt us—or people who are afraid of seeing us hurt again—will help us find reasons to blame ourselves. But that whole process is based on a lie. We're never responsible for what other people do to us.

An act of rape is always the responsibility of the rapist. Of course, knowing that fact won't be of any help to the woman who's about to step into a car with a man who has a tendency to rape. What she needs at that moment is a combination of awareness, knowledge, and skills. She needs to be aware of any signals the man is sending out, and of her "gut" feelings about those signals. She needs to know the warning signs of rape. And most of all, she needs skills that will help her stay out of that car. At that moment, she's responsible for her own protection because there's no one else around who can help her.

Some people say that women shouldn't have to change their lifestyles in any way because of the threat of rape. That's true. Rape shouldn't exist, either. But it does. If you lived in a high-crime area, with the possibility of being hit by stray bullets at any time of the day or night, wouldn't you change your lifestyle to avoid the bullets? That wouldn't make it your fault if you were shot. But being careful might make your life longer and less painful.

Whose Responsibility Is Rape?

- Rape is the responsibility of the person who commits it.
- Self-protection is the responsibility of each woman and man.
- Sexual respect, safety, and dignity are the responsibility of all of us, together.

Here's a suggestion: While you're reading or talking about this book, please take the idea of responsibility and separate it completely from the idea of blame. Put the word "blame" aside for a while, in a part of your brain where it won't get in the way. You can always pull it out later, if you need it. The idea of blame doesn't have much practical use anyway, except in court. And divide responsibility up into many little pieces, so each person can be responsible for his or her actions without being responsible for what other people do. It might make it easier to see which choices and responsibilities are yours, and to think of yourself as a "choice maker."

There's also another kind of responsibility, like another layer that lies on top of all our individual pieces of responsibility. It's called collective responsibility. That means that all of us, together, have a responsibility to try to make our world a safe, respectful, loving place where people can live in dignity and freedom. It means that sexual force and manipulation—as symptoms of the larger problems that we all share—are everyone's responsibility.

That responsibility calls us—women and men—to try to understand and accept one another. It calls us to listen to one another, communicate honestly, and care about what others feel. It calls us to avoid making sexist judgments and remarks, whether the objects of those remarks are male or female. It calls us to cross gender lines, to support and defend one another.

Our responsibility challenges us to let go of the old, destructive model of relationship—not only for our own sake, but for the sake of the children who watch our example. They're as innocent, and as vulnerable, as we ever were.

Who's Worth Protecting?

Just who or what do the authors believe is "worth protecting"? First, every human being is worth protecting from manipulation and violence—whether or not we feel like we're worth it. Human dignity, freedom, and well-being are worth protecting, even if we have to go to a lot of trouble to do it. And true friendship between men and women is worth protecting, even though the popular culture seems determined to convince us that we're enemies.

There will always be rapists. A certain number of people will be raped in dating relationships no matter how good their awareness, skills, and attitudes are. They'll be fooled completely, tricked into situations where they can't escape or fight back. And some people will rape and manipulate no matter how well they understand their choices and responsibilities. Some people of both genders don't—and won't—care about the effects of their actions on others or themselves.

But many more men and women will be able to understand these problems, avoid them in the future, heal their wounds, learn new skills, and make a commitment to healthy, respectful relationships. We'll learn to let the old relationship model fall away as we experience more and more of the benefits of the new model. And many young people will be able to take on different ways of thinking and relating—and so avoid all that pain and confusion.

It's worth the effort. We're *all* worth protecting.

Notes

1. The Bibliography lists some good sources of statistics on date rape and acquaintance rape. For example, *I Never Called It Rape* by Robin Warshaw gives a thorough introduction to the subject. In the landmark study documented in that book, one in four women reported having been raped or subjected to attempted rape; 84 percent of the women who were raped knew their attackers; and 57 percent of the rapes happened on dates. *Acquaintance Rape: The Hidden Crime,* edited by Andrea Parrot and Laurie Bechhofer, also provides a large selection of research on the subject from a feminist perspective.

Journal Questions

1. Has anyone ever used guilt, sympathy, social pressure, or trickery to talk you into sexual acts you didn't want—or have you used those techniques on another person? How important does that incident seem to you when you think about it?

2. Have you ever been forced to do something sexual you didn't freely choose to do—or forced someone else to do something sexual? Did you think of this as rape?

3. Have you ever used sexual attraction to get something from someone, gain power, or make up for feelings of inadequacy?

4. Have you ever thought of or defined yourself as a victim? What were or are your emotional reactions to those thoughts? What effects might those emotional reactions have had on your actions?

5. How often do you notice—or even look for—choice points in the course of your daily life?

6. What are your definitions of "blame" and "responsibility"? How easy or hard is it to think of one without the other? If you tend to combine them, where might you have learned to do that?

PART II

What
We Find

CHAPTER 2

A Losing Battle

The so-called battle of the sexes is a battle that no one wins. But it's all around us all the time, in subtle and not-so-subtle forms.

Watching a movie, we can always tell which man and woman are going to "fall in love." They're the ones who fight like crazy from the moment they meet. They scheme and lie to one another. They act as if they hate each other. The last thing they'd do would be to admit what they really want, or how they really feel.

Of course, they don't want the same thing. One—usually the woman—wants marriage and babies, and the other wants a "good time" —in other words, sex without commitment. The whole point is to trick the other into giving them what they want without telling the other about it. If they were honest, that would spoil the excitement and the mystery. As a result, they're both going crazy. We've learned to recognize that as a sure sign of being in love.

When they do fall, it's with an all-consuming passion that both hurls them toward one another and draws battle lines between them. Their first kiss is an attack, and the moment of truth comes when the heroine stops struggling.

They've learned to mistake fear for excitement, confusion for mystery, anger for passion, pleasure for happiness, and dependence for love. So have many of us. As a society we're addicted to conflict, blame, and sensationalism. Honesty and cooperation seem boring by comparison.

Why Haven't Things Changed?

Many hoped that the changes in women's and men's roles and sexual customs over the past few decades might bring a truce. In many cases, though, they seem to have made the battle more intense for a while. The rules that cover sexual and romantic expectations were confusing and conflicted before those changes began. Now they're even more confusing and conflicted. The old, destructive model of relationship hasn't been weakened by the changes in women's and men's roles—because that model thrives on confusion and conflict.

We've learned to mistake fear for excitement, confusion for mystery, anger for passion, pleasure for happiness, and dependence for love.

When we hear of an incident—let's say a woman accuses a man of date rape and it's her word against his—we think immediately about what he might have done to her, or what she might have done to make him think she wanted him. We think about what's wrong with men, or what's wrong with women. But unless we think about what all of us are doing—and how it all fits together—we're off track. Unless we understand all the forces that led to the incident, we can't hope to keep it from happening again.

Effects of the Old Model

To see a few of those forces at work, look at the fictional case of Don and Sandy. These two young people have been raised on the old relationship model. Their training as a man and a woman has been typical, but it will backfire when they're brought together. Here you'll see some of the confusion, misunderstanding, and pain that sometimes follow when women and men are trained to think of one another as "things" to be won or lost, rather than as friends.

Don

All his life Don has tried to figure out what was expected of him so that he could do it. It hasn't been easy. The expectations have changed from person to person, and from minute to minute. He felt there were all kinds of secret rules that everybody else knew but nobody wanted to tell him.

Sometimes Don's father treated him like he was in boot camp, even when he was a little kid. He'd play too rough and yell at Don if he cried. He'd expect perfect grades and winning scores at games. The only emotion he ever showed was anger. Don learned early that being tough was the only way to go.

When he was a child Don kept hearing that men and women were supposed to be equal partners, but his parents didn't act as if that were true. They acted like his father was boss. He figured his dad was a good father because he had a good job and made good money.

Then when Don was ten, a lot of the industry in the area shut down, and his father couldn't find a job for a year. After that, he had to work more hours for a lot less pay. His mother got a job, too. She appeared to enjoy it, but his father didn't like the fact that she was working. It made it harder for her to take care of her husband and kids, and she didn't keep the house as clean. That was when his parents started fighting all the time. He hated to hear them fight, but by then he was pretty good at tuning them out.

When Don was fourteen his father warned him that women were going to try to trap him into marriage. He said Don could mess around and have his fun, but that he should put off getting married until he found the right woman. Don wondered if his mother was the right woman for his dad, or if she'd trapped him. He didn't ask.

Television taught Don that women were either "easy" or "prissy," and that real sexual satisfaction was always the result of a struggle—a struggle that the man had to win. The power to win came from money, fame, and physical strength. Power was always power over someone else. The reward for power and conquest was to be recognized as a "real man." Somehow that meant he'd get just what he needed to survive.

In their teens, Don's buddies traded details of their sexual conquests as if they were baseball cards. They were proud of their ability to be "strong." Being strong meant not having any emotions—except anger, of course—and not paying attention to other people's emotions. When Don used to cry he felt deeply ashamed, so he learned to get angry instead.

He knew that his "softer" feelings for a girl would give her power over him. So he learned to think of girls and women as objects. He decided just to get what he wanted and avoid their traps. He felt they had too much power. They had the power to make him want them and then to say no. He resented that power. He feared being turned down by women, because he would feel humiliated. It would mean that he was somehow less than a "real man."

The more Don heard about women wanting to be treated as equals, the more he resented them. He believed they wanted to get new advantages but still keep the old ones. He kept hearing that women wanted men to be more gentle and sensitive, but most of the women he knew tended to turn down the more sensitive men in favor of more dominant, "macho" men. When he talked to women he was always on his guard. Whatever way he acted with them, he risked being criticized—by them or by his male friends.

Some of the Rules that Many Men Learn

- You have to win.
- Be tough: don't show any emotion except anger.
- Get money and power.
- A woman should take care of your sexual and emotional needs.
- Don't get trapped by the wrong woman.
- You have a right to sex if you spend a lot of money.
- You have to prove your manhood by "conquering" women.

Some of the Rules that Many Women Learn

- Don't be too assertive or make a fuss: be a lady.
- Don't show anger, especially with a nice guy.
- You need to "catch" a man who'll take care of you financially.
- It's your job to take care of men's sexual and emotional needs.
- If a man spends a lot of money on you, you owe him sex.
- It's a man's job to try to get sex, and your job to stop him.

At the age of twenty-four, Don is confused, frustrated, and angry. He's been working for the same company for four years. He recently put in for a promotion, but a woman from outside the company was hired instead, and now he's going to report to her. He had to get all dressed up today for a big meeting to hear about the changes she plans to make. He feels like a monkey in a three-piece suit. If he could recognize and tell you how he feels, he'd say he feels scared and powerless.

41

It's not okay to feel that way, though, so he just knows he's angry.

It's happy hour, and Don is sitting in a neighborhood bar with some friends. He's covering up his shaky feelings with shots and beers, and with funny stories about how he messed with his new boss's head today.

Don is sitting next to Sandy, a young woman he's seen around for a couple of months. There's something about her that seems attractive to him tonight, and he's been buying her drinks. She's been letting him. He's even been putting his arm around her shoulder a little bit, and a couple of times he put his hand on her thigh. She acted as if she didn't notice, and kept listening to him and nodding. He's keeping her laughing, and he's wondering what approach would be the best one to get her in bed tonight.

Sandy

Like Don, Sandy was well trained in the ways of power and powerlessness. As a child, she watched as her mother found sneaky ways around her domineering alcoholic father's rule. Her mother appeared unhappy in the relationship, but she also seemed terrified of losing it. She took good care of her husband and blamed herself whenever things went wrong. Sandy loved her father, but she also feared him. She tiptoed around when he was home.

Sandy watched some of the same TV shows Don watched as a child and learned from them that there are two kinds of men: dangerous and boring. She also learned that sexual attractiveness makes a woman both more powerful and more vulnerable. She grew up feeling ugly and wanting more than anything else to be beautiful. If she were beautiful, she could attract a man who would marry her and take care of her. Then she'd be happy.

In her family and school, girls weren't encouraged to get angry and show their anger. There were all kinds of subtle punishments for doing that. Her parents and teachers told her to "act like a lady." Of course, if she did she got laughed at by her classmates. There was no choice that would please everybody, and Sandy desperately wanted to please everybody.

When she was in her teens, Sandy's friends knew all about "the rules" that governed dating and relationships. The trouble was that the rules sometimes contradicted one another. It was important to make a boy want her—there was power in that—but if she had sex with him, she would give away that power.

If a guy was nice and respectable, she had to be nice to him. She also had to trust him. It would be insulting to him if she didn't. Nice guys didn't do bad things. If a man used force on her in a sexual situation, she was supposed to stop him. But, of course, he was just doing what was in his nature to do.

If a man didn't spend a lot of money on a woman, that meant he didn't value her very highly—or he was cheap or broke. But if he did spend a lot of money on her, she owed him sex. If she had sex too soon, she'd be labeled a "tramp" and lose her value as a potential wife. If she was in love, though—and he was in love with her—it might be okay to have sex, as long as she made him wait long enough for it.

It was all pretty confusing, but one thing was clear: It was the guy's job to try to get sex from her, and her job to keep him from getting it. Her other job was to "catch" a husband. As they grew up, Sandy and her friends learned a subtle sort of calculus—juggling all those factors to figure out what was okay and what was expected. As she entered her twenties, Sandy found that calculus harder and harder to do. She sometimes felt guilty if she said no—but just as guilty if she said yes.

All her life Sandy had heard people talk about women's equality and women's rights. She liked the idea, but somehow her thoughts on that subject didn't change the beliefs about sex she'd grown up with—or the behavior that resulted. For one thing, she didn't really feel equal to anyone. Most of the time she felt stupid and boring, and she had a hard time sticking up for herself. Sometimes she felt helpless and trapped. The idea of equality just set up more goals that she felt she couldn't reach.

Sandy is attracted to Don. He's been buying her drinks for a couple of hours now. He's good looking and funny, but she feels like there's something a little strange about him, almost a violence riding just under the surface. She tells herself there's nothing to worry about. She's seen him around for a couple of months, and they have friends in common. And he's very well dressed tonight, so he probably has a good job. He's probably okay.

He's also been asking her questions about herself, and acting as if he's interested in her answers. She's been telling him about her childhood and some of the problems in her family. He really seems to care.

She hasn't even thought about the possibility of having sex with him tonight. She felt a little nervous when he put his hand on her thigh, but she didn't want to offend him by saying something, so she ignored it. It seems like forever since an attractive man paid any attention to her. She feels attractive for the first time in a long time.

What Happens Next?

Don and Sandy are getting ready to leave the bar together. Any number of things might happen after that. They'll most likely get some dinner and more drinks, then end up alone together, at his place or hers. They'll do some exploratory necking and petting. If he tries to go farther, she'll probably try to stop him, and he'll do his best to get her to give in.

She might give in, feeling as if she owes him sex—or afraid of making him angry. She might decide he's too drunk to stop. Or she might pass out, and he might have sex with her anyway. Neither one would realize it, but that would be rape.

On the other hand, she might hold her ground and say no. In that case, will he just go home—feeling angry and insulted? Or will all his pent-up anger and frustrations take over, and will he try to "take" what he feels is due to him?

If he does, will she fight back? She'll probably struggle, but will she be willing to hurt him, or will she be afraid of his reaction? Will she be willing to scream, or afraid of what the neighbors might think? If she does fight back, will she have the strength or the skills to win?

> **If we were more aware of how we've been "programmed," we might find out who we really are. Both men and women might choose sexual safety and respect.**

The effects might be anywhere from mild to horrible. He might go home frustrated and angry. She might have sex against her true wishes, and her negative feelings about herself would be sure to increase. She might be raped, and so begin a long period of fear, depression, and self-hatred. He might lose his temper and hit her. She might get pregnant. Either one of them might end up with HIV/AIDS or another disease. Someone's life could be changed permanently. Someone's life could be lost.

The tragedy is that all these effects are common. The most frustrating part is that in many cases the outcome could have been prevented. If the people involved were more aware of the beliefs and expectations that were "programmed" into them in childhood, they might be able to sort out who they really were and what they really wanted. Men might not choose violence, and both partners might choose self-protection. People might choose honest communication and friendship instead of manipulation.

Effects of the New Model

In an ideal world, both Don and Sandy would have grown up watching their parents support one another, enjoy one another's company, and work together to solve problems peacefully. They would have known deep in their hearts that their parents were true friends. Over the years their parents would have told them the secret—how to stay friends with a partner despite the stress and problems that are sure to arise.

Television would have shown them how interesting and challenging life can be when people's time and energy aren't taken up in anxiety and meaningless conflict. It would have shown them how boring those self-destructive patterns can be after a while. They would have watched love grow slowly out of friendship.

Family members, friends, schools, the media, and the community as a whole would have reminded them over and over that they're worthwhile—and worthy of love— exactly as they are. They would have come to love and respect themselves, and have no need to feel "better than" or "worse than" anyone else.

Growing up with their friends, they wouldn't have spent all that time talking about how to get what they wanted from members of the opposite sex. Instead, they would have focused on figuring out who they were and what they really wanted for their own lives. They would have realized that they didn't need to try to use other people to fill up the holes in their lives and their images of themselves.

46

When they did talk about the opposite sex, it would be to share their growing understanding of how men and women are different—and how we're alike. They would have talked about the hopes, dreams, and fears we all have in common, and explored the differences in the way we communicate.[1]

Neither of them would have felt helpless. If they believed in a higher power (for example, a concept of God, Allah, spirituality, etc.), they would have felt the strength, care, and comfort of that power running through them all the time. But even if they hadn't believed in a higher power, they would have believed in themselves. They would have known that problems have solutions and people have options.

> **Once we let go of the drama, we can fill our lives with things that really mean something to us.**

When Don and Sandy met, they wouldn't have been sizing one another up as potential sources of sex, commitment, power, or self-worth. Instead, they would have focused on one thing: On that evening they had an opportunity to begin to know another human being. Maybe they'd turn out to be friends, and maybe not. Either way, they'd have a chance to exchange some stories, some strength, and some humor. That exchange might help them get to know themselves a little better and deal a little better with the pressures in their lives.

If they found out that they had enough things in common and enjoyed one another's company, they might have made an arrangement to go out together or to meet again another day. They might have talked about what they wanted in a partner or a relationship, or they might have waited until they knew each other better. But whatever they decided to do, it would have been because both people honestly and freely chose to do it.

Does this sound boring to you? If it does, it might be because you were raised on the old model of relationship, in the same conflict-filled, sensation-driven world as most of us. But think of this: If you've lived your life in drama after drama, what would happen if that drama were taken away? Would there be a big hole where it used to be, or would other things slowly take its place? Isn't there a chance those other things might be more interesting, have more variety, and really set you free?

It's worth a try.

Notes

1. For more information on the differences between the communication styles of women and men, you might start with *You Just Don't Understand* by Deborah Tannen; *Men, Women, and Aggression,* by Anne Campbell; John Gray's *Men Are From Mars, Women Are From Venus;* Naireh and Smith's *Why Can't Men Open Up?*; or "Sex, Lies, and Dating," by Neil Chesanow in *New Woman* magazine. See the Bibliography for a more complete listing.

Journal Questions

1. How many things have you seen or heard in the past two days that directly or indirectly show conflict or one-upmanship between women and men? (These might be jokes, sarcastic comments, or scenes from TV, movies, or books.) You might try making a list of them for a day.

2. How much of Don's and Sandy's early training sounded familiar to you, from your own life or the lives of people you know?

3. What do you think is the most likely outcome of Don and Sandy's evening together? What makes you choose this possibility over the others?

4. What dreams or ideas do you have for your life that you've never had the time or energy to try? Is it possible that a different approach to intimate relationships might leave you with a little more room to explore your own possibilities?

5. What are "the rules"? Is there one set of rules that covers dating, sex, and relationships? Are you at all confused about the rules?

CHAPTER 3

The Old Model of Relationship

It's time to take a closer look at the old model of relationship. Sexual force and manipulation aren't the only problems that often have their roots in this model. Sexual harassment, domestic violence, jealousy, and many problems that lead to the breakup of relationships can also be offshoots of the old model.

It helps to think of this model as a circle or "cycle" that always leads us back where it started. The main thing about a cycle is that it keeps itself going. Every point along the way pushes us off toward the next point—until we end up at the beginning again. Then we start our next round.

Once we're in a cycle, it's hard to get out of it—or to stop what's happening. The faster the cycle goes, the more we're pulled back into it. And the more we spin, the harder it is to keep our balance.

In the old model of relationship, both partners are spinning in the same circle. We may be taking on different roles, but it's the same drama. And even when we act in opposite ways, our actions often come from—or lead to—the same kinds of mixed-up beliefs, thoughts, and emotions.

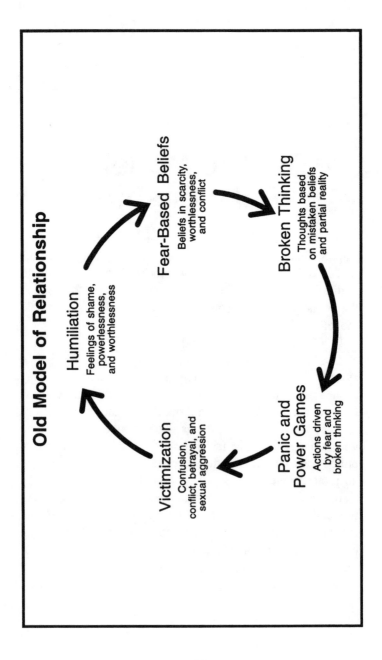

Old Model of Relationship

Fear-Based Beliefs
Beliefs in scarcity, worthlessness, and conflict

Broken Thinking
Thoughts based on mistaken beliefs and partial reality

Panic and Power Games
Actions driven by fear and broken thinking

Victimization
Confusion, conflict, betrayal, and sexual aggression

Humiliation
Feelings of shame, powerlessness, and worthlessness

This figure shows how the old model of relationship flows. The five points or "phases" of the cycle are: (1) humiliation, (2) fear-based beliefs, (3) broken thinking, (4) panic and power games, and (5) victimization. Here's how the cycle works:

Phase One: Humiliation

Humiliation is an experience of deep shame, a reaction to pain. It usually follows some kind of attack, or something we feel is an attack. It might be something painful that someone says or does to us. It might be the moment we notice that we're different from others, or that we don't appear to have what they have.

Humiliation often includes being seen by others and having them see our shame. We look into their eyes and think we see that we're worthless—and we believe it. We feel lost, broken, and terrified. Humiliation also includes our feeling of power-lessness when we can't stop the attack or make the pain and shame go away.

Most of us react to feelings of fear and worthlessness by giving up or by striking out at others.

For most people who live in the old model, the feeling of deep-down humiliation started in childhood. It might have begun with physical, sexual, or emotional abuse by a parent, family member, or teacher. It might have started with teasing from other children, parents, or teachers. It might have come from feeling the judgment of others because of our race, culture, gender, disability, or sexual orientation. Humiliation might have been a way of life in a family troubled by poverty, addiction, constant conflict, or mental illness.

As the feelings of fear and worthlessness dug in, most of us learned to react in one of two ways. Either we learned to give up and give in, or we learned to strike out at others. The feelings of fear and worthlessness didn't go away. We just got used to them, or covered them up so we wouldn't know they were there.

For example, Don in chapter two learned to get tough. He took his father's bullying and put on a crust of anger that he thought would protect him. He felt his father's shame when his father lost his job and his mother started working. It's that shame that still threatens him, under the surface, now that his new female supervisor has been hired for the job he wanted.

Sandy reacted to her father's threats by tiptoeing around the house when he was home. She took on her mother's feelings of shame and fear. She tried to disappear and learned to put up with feeling dull, confused, and unattractive. It's those feelings that drew her toward Don that night.

Both Don and Sandy decided early in life that they were basically worthless and powerless. Both were angry about that, but Don turned his anger outward, while Sandy turned hers back on herself. Both choices lead to the second phase: fear-based beliefs.

Phase Two: Fear-Based Beliefs

Whether we decide to turn our anger inward or outward, the feelings underneath it are the same. Most people leave the humiliation stage filled with feelings of worthlessness and powerlessness. Without even knowing it, we've made a commitment to fear. Our world is now a dangerous place where people get attacked. Whether we've taken on the role of Little Red Riding Hood or the Big Bad Wolf, we're in the same forest full of spooky trees.

There are many kinds of beliefs that come out of this fear. Different people learn and choose different beliefs. It depends on our experiences, what we hear, and what fits in best with our basic nature as people. But here are some of the fear-based beliefs that often lead us to use sexual force or manipulation—or keep us from protecting ourselves from other people's force or manipulation:

1. *"I'm incomplete."* There's something missing in me, and I need someone or something to complete me. I have to prove myself. If I'm a man, I need to prove my manhood by getting women to have sex with me, by being strong and tough, or by making a lot of money. If I'm a woman, I need to complete myself by finding the right man, by being glamorous and beautiful, or by being famous and successful.

2. *"There's not enough to go around."* I'm in danger of not getting what I want or need to complete me, because there aren't enough of the right kinds of "things" (women, men, jobs, opportunities, etc.) to go around. If I don't get what I want, I'll stay incomplete and worthless.

3. *"I don't matter."* What I want doesn't matter. What I don't want doesn't matter. What happens to me doesn't matter. I don't deserve to be treated well, or to have my wants, needs, or limits respected. Or maybe it's wrong for me to want anything at all, so whatever I want must be wrong. I don't deserve it.

4. *"I have to think the best of people."* If people are nice and respectable, it's not nice to think bad thoughts about them. For example, it's not nice to think that nice people might try to force or manipulate me into having sex. So I shouldn't insult them by taking steps to make sure I'm safe.

5. *"Men and women are at war."* This person is my enemy. If I'm a man, women have all the power, because they have the power to say no. If I'm a woman, men have all the power, and they want to hurt women. So I have to trick this person into giving me what I want or need, or else he or she will trick me and humiliate me. That's just the way it is.

6. *"I'm a victim."* I don't have any choice in the matter. Once a victim, always a victim. There's only one way to keep from being a victim, and that's to hurt other people. They'd do it to me, so I have to do it to them first. I'm not responsible for what I do. They made me do it.

Fear-Based Beliefs
1. I'm incomplete.
2. There's not enough to go around.
3. I don't matter.
4. I have to think the best of people.
5. Men and women are at war.
6. I'm a victim.

In our example from the last chapter, both Don and Sandy were raised to believe that they were incomplete. They were raised to think about how to "get" someone of the opposite sex, so they could fill that incompleteness. Sandy grew up believing she didn't matter. Now she ignores her feeling that something isn't right about Don, because he's well dressed and he's a friend of friends. That makes him a nice person, and it wouldn't be nice to question his motives.

Both Don and Sandy grew up believing that men and women are enemies, and they both believe they're victims. Sandy's reaction to Don's touching her thigh is to let him do what he wants, as if she has no power to stop him. And Don feels victimized by his new supervisor. He's reacting to that by wanting to feel powerful with Sandy.

Of course, neither of them is aware of these old beliefs. But that doesn't make the old beliefs any less powerful. If anything, it makes them more powerful. The beliefs lead into certain ways of thinking, the next phase of our cycle.

Phase Three: Broken Thinking

This phase is called "broken thinking" because our thoughts are based on mistaken beliefs. Our focus on our chosen role as victim or victimizer has blocked out many important perceptions and choices. Our thought processes, which should be based on reality as a whole, are messed up because we're seeing only part of the truth.

The broken-thinking phase includes many different kinds of thinking. The six listed here follow the fear-based beliefs described in the last phase:

1. *Commodity thinking.* This is seeing other people as things, to be won or lost. Remember, I've decided I'm incomplete, and other people can complete me. If I'm a man, I need a woman for sex. If I'm a woman, I need a man for commitment and security. So I keep thinking about whether or not I can use this person to fill my need. If he or she can't help complete me in the right way, then this person is of no use to me.

2. *Scarcity thinking.* Because I don't believe there's enough to go around, I'm seeing other people not only as things but also as things that are hard to find. This may be the last man or woman who's ever attracted to me. I'd better get what I want or need now, at all costs. So I also learn to see people of my own sex as competition.

3. *Lack of self-knowledge.* If it doesn't matter what I want or don't want—or if what I want is always going to be wrong—then why bother asking myself what I want or don't want with this particular person? I go into situations not even knowing what my sexual desires or limits are.

4. *Exception thinking.* I know that some men rape and manipulate women, but this guy is nice and respectable. He's different. I know that many women get offended if men get aggressive with them, but this one is different. She's hot for me!

5. *Attack thinking.* I can't be honest with this person, because we're at war as men and women. He or she has all the power, so I have to be sneaky. If I want sex, I have to hide my true motives, because otherwise I'll be rejected. If he does something inappropriate, I have to presume that he wants to hurt me. I have to teach him or her a lesson.

6. *Ignoring choices and responsibilities.* If I'm a helpless victim, then it doesn't even occur to me that I have other choices or the power to make them. So I don't notice my "choice points"—times when I might do things to protect myself or keep the situation from going bad. And it doesn't even occur to me to try to think of other options. I feel trapped. I think of everything that happens to me as being caused by outside forces. I don't take responsibility for my own actions.

Fear-Based Beliefs	Broken Thinking
1. I'm incomplete.	Commodity thinking
2. There's not enough to go around.	Scarcity thinking
3. I don't matter.	Lack of self-knowledge
4. I have to think the best of people	Exception thinking
5. Men and women are at war.	Attack thinking
6. I'm a victim.	Ignoring choices and responsibilities

Both Don and Sandy have been trained in the ways of commodity thinking and scarcity thinking. There's a sense of urgency about Don's mood, and Sandy isn't questioning things. She's just relieved to feel attractive for the first time in a long while.

Sandy hasn't asked herself whether or not she might want to be sexually involved with Don. She's generally confused about the whole subject of sex. She has felt a little uncomfortable with Don, but she hasn't set any limits or talked about what she does or doesn't want. It doesn't seem necessary with a nice guy like him. And Don isn't even questioning his desire to "score" with Sandy tonight. It's as if he doesn't know he has a choice.

Each of them has already decided that the other one has all the power. Don has been trained to resent the fact that Sandy has the power to say no. And Sandy's been trained to accept the fact that Don has the power to decide what happens. Of course, with a nice guy like Don that shouldn't be a problem.

These broken ways of thinking lead to a jumble of confused feelings and careless or dishonest words and actions. They lead us to the next phase: panic and power games.

Phase Four: Panic and Power Games

In this phase we start to act on our fear-based beliefs and thought patterns. Because we're driven by fear, we tend to panic and to think in terms of power. Here are some of the most common ways of acting out our fears in relationships. Again, these are numbered to match the beliefs and thoughts that lead to them:

1. *Trying to control the outcome.* If I need this person to complete me—and I'm out to "win" him or her—then I have to make sure this relationship develops in a certain way. I have to manipulate events. I can't possibly be honest. I can't be myself. I have to impress this person by being the

person he or she seems to want me to be. Our involvement is based on control moves.

2. *Rushing things.* If this might be my last chance (to find a partner for sex or commitment, etc.), then I can't let this chance slip through my hands. I need to make it happen. I can't just wait to find out how it will turn out. I have to make things move as quickly as possible. I want to get very close, very quickly. So I might tell this person intimate things about me when I haven't known him or her very long. I mistake anxiety for excitement.

3. *Not communicating wants, needs, limits, and expectations.* I'm not really clear in my own mind about what I want or don't want, and what my limits are. So I don't communicate my wants, needs, limits, and expectations clearly to this person. I might send hints, give double messages, or say nothing at all. But I don't say what I mean in clear, direct words. I expect this person to read my mind.

4. *Not being careful.* I've already decided that the rules of being careful don't apply to this situation, because this is different. So even if I have skills for setting limits, asking permission, or keeping out of dangerous areas, I don't use them. I might find myself getting physical without making sure it's okay to do that. Or I might find myself alone with the wrong man on a deserted beach, miles away from other people.

5. *Power games.* Once I've decided I can't be honest or up-front with this person, I have to use other ways of getting my way. I might flirt with someone I'm not really interested in, just to see if I can get him or her interested. I might use manipulation or force to get sex. I might use guilt or sympathy to get my way.

6. *Compulsion.* I feel I have no choices, and so feel forced to do what I do. I might feel as if I have to use all my tricks and traps to get someone into bed. Or I might feel as if I can't say no—and get out of the situation—when someone is pushing me. If I'm a man, I might think I've reached the "point of no return," and feel as if I can't stop. I might even believe I'm being forced to use force. If someone's using force on me, I might believe I can't scream or fight back.

Fear-Based Beliefs	Broken Thinking	Panic and Power Games
1. I'm incomplete.	Commodity thinking	Trying to control the outcome
2. There's not enough to go around.	Scarcity thinking	Rushing things
3. I don't matter.	Lack of self-knowledge	Not communicating wants, needs, expectations, and limits
4. I have to think the best of people.	Exception thinking	Not being careful
5. Men and women are at war.	Attack thinking	Power games
6. I'm a victim.	Ignoring choices	Compulsion

In our example of Don and Sandy, Don appears to be putting on a false self to impress Sandy. He wants to control her reaction to him. He's feeling hurt and scared from his experiences at work, but he's making a big joke of it, and making it sound like he got the best of his supervisor.

Sandy has also moved quickly into saying very personal things about her childhood, and Don has been encouraging her. Each one of them has a different outcome in mind, and each one is doing his or her best to bring the evening in line with that outcome.

Because we're not sure what happens to Sandy and Don after they leave the bar, it's hard to tell how hard this phase will hit them. But they've been pushed to this phase with all the force of the first three phases, so the chances are they'll get in some kind of trouble in the final phase: victimization.

Phase Five: Victimization

This is the phase where people get hurt. It's the phase where potential friendships "blow up" because people aren't being themselves. In many cases both people feel betrayed because neither of them was saying what he or she expected—and they turned out to be expecting different things.

In this phase, many people who've shared their deepest secrets turn out to be just looking for a good time. They were trying to create a false sense of closeness so they could use manipulation or force to get what they wanted. What they wanted might have been sex, money, opportunities, or any combination of these. Here the other partner's sense of betrayal reaches deep into his or her private experiences and emotions.

This is also the phase where some men who believed they were just having "rough sex"—or acting out a fantasy—find out that what they did was called rape. And some men who had no clue that the woman wasn't willing to have sex find themselves accused of raping her.

In many cases both people feel betrayed because neither of them was saying what he or she expected—and they turned out to be expecting different things.

In this phase some people are raped, beaten, even killed by people they trusted. The feelings of betrayal can be worse than anyone can imagine who hasn't had the experience. The painful, fearful effects of rape can last for many years. And the ones who commit these crimes often find their own pain, guilt, and fear increasing. An attack on another always becomes an attack on ourselves in time. The world becomes more frightening. We become victims of our own cruelty.

Confused by the reality of all these kinds of victimization, women and men become more and more confused. We're confused about sexuality, relationships, safety, ourselves, our responsibilities, and one another. We've been taught to look in dating relationships for things like love, desire, intimacy, confidence, self-worth, and satisfaction. But all these things have been ground up in the old model, over and over again.

We see what we've done—and what's been done to us—and once again we feel pain, worthlessness, and powerlessness. We're thrown back into the humiliation phase, and the cycle begins again.

Jumping Models

All this might sound hopeless if it weren't for the possibility of doing things differently—and getting different results. There's a new model of relationship that's the exact opposite of this one. It's possible to jump from one model to the other at any phase. It takes effort, and it often takes help. But it is possible.

Some people reach a point where they've simply had enough pain and humiliation. In the chemical dependency field people talk about "hitting bottom." "Bottom" is the place where the pain of going through the same thing over and over grows stronger than the fear of changing. It's different for each person.

Some people have to lose almost everything before they give up and get help for their problems. Others just need a few bad experiences—plus an idea of how bad it will get if they don't take steps to change. Still others keep on destroying themselves until they die. And then there are those who see what their parents and friends are going through and decide not to try alcohol or other drugs at all.

It's like that with the old model of relationship. We might not let it go until we've raped someone or been raped, landed in the hospital or prison, picked up HIV (the virus that causes AIDS), or just grown bitter and cynical. Or we can look honestly at our patterns of dating and relationships, and see the anger, anxiety, and pain they've caused. We can decide that we don't have to go through that any more, or put anyone else through it. A popular definition of insanity is "doing the same thing over and over again and expecting different results." We can declare ourselves sane.

Transformation

Hitting bottom, wherever that bottom turns out to be, can be the first step in a process of transformation. Our beliefs about ourselves, our thought patterns, our actions, and our lives can change in ways we never thought possible. Obviously it takes work and it takes help. Some people do the work more quickly or slowly than others. And the help we need for transformation can come from different places. But we're all changed if we let the transformation process happen.

In the pain of hitting bottom, we develop a strong desire not to get hurt anymore or to hurt anyone else. We decide to stop reacting to humiliation by caving in or striking out at others. It didn't work. It always led to more humiliation. What's left? Let's call it humility.

Humility is an old word that people often mistake for a false sense of not being important. That's not how the word started out, though. Real humility is an honest and accurate knowledge of our true worth—no more and no less. It's being "teachable"—being willing to look at our mistakes and our successes honestly, ready to learn from both. It's having an open mind and being willing to accept help.

> **We decide to stop reacting to humiliation by caving in or striking out at others. It didn't work. It always led to more humiliation.**

Transformation includes a lot of learning. We need to change our beliefs about ourselves and others. We need to learn and practice skills that will keep us safe and help us respect others' safety. We need to learn to recognize our choices and take responsibility for our actions and their effects. We need to get help in healing our wounds, old and new. And we need to decide that we deserve happy and peaceful lives. As you can imagine, this process can take quite a while.

Being Honest About Payoffs

Obviously there's been some kind of "payoff"—some kind of reward for our pain in the old model—or we wouldn't have kept traveling this circle over and over again. Maybe it's been comforting to know exactly what our roles were, even if those roles have been painful to us or others. Maybe we're afraid of getting to know ourselves too well, for fear of what we'll find. If we take away our destructive and self-destructive beliefs, thoughts, and actions, will we ever be able to replace them? Or will we just be bored for the rest of our lives?

We might be afraid of changing our beliefs about ourselves, other people, and sexuality. We might feel like we're not being loyal to the people who taught us those beliefs or the culture that played them over and over again in our ears. It helps to figure out what our payoffs have been so we can begin to let go of them.

Hope

All the pain in the world wouldn't help us change if we didn't also have a handle on hope. That's what the next chapter is for. It outlines the new model of relationship, holding it up to the old one and inviting us to jump.

Usually we'll need help, but help is available in many forms. Most of us have friends who appear to have respectful friendships with the people they date. We can ask them for their feedback and support. And if we're in touch with inner sources of spiritual strength, we can find amazing results when we tap into those sources.

There are also therapists, counseling programs, men's groups, women's groups, teens' groups, Twelve-Step groups, and other mutual-help groups for face-to-face support. We can even start groups to work on these issues. The *Worth Protecting* workbook is a good place to start, with exercises for groups and individuals based on the models in this book.

There's hope and there's help. Let's look at the new model to see if it's worth jumping.

Journal Questions

1. Everyone has experienced humiliation. What's your most common reaction to feelings of humiliation? Do you strike out or retreat inside yourself? Do you react in another way?

2. Did any of the fear-based beliefs sound familiar to you from your own life? How might these beliefs have affected the process of getting to know people you were interested in dating?

3. Did any of the examples of broken thinking sound familiar to you from your own life? Can you think of any others along the same lines? How might these kinds of thoughts affect the way you feel?

4. When you're in new or ongoing relationships, do you feel in balance or a little off balance? How do you handle the power issue: Do you feel as if you have more power, your partner has more power, or it's equal?

5. Do any of the examples of panic and power games sound familiar to you?

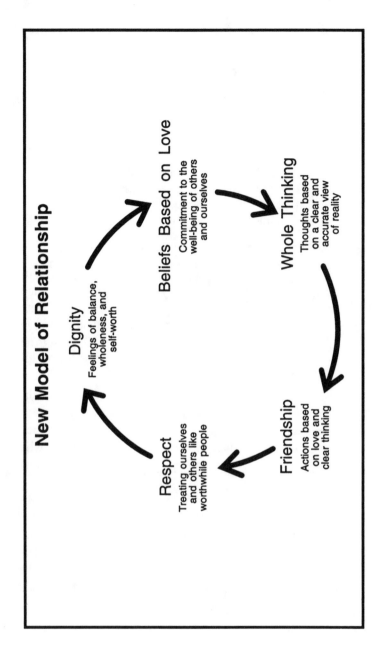

New Model of Relationship

Beliefs Based on Love
Commitment to the well-being of others and ourselves

Whole Thinking
Thoughts based on a clear and accurate view of reality

Friendship
Actions based on love and clear thinking

Respect
Treating ourselves and others like worthwhile people

Dignity
Feelings of balance, wholeness, and self-worth

CHAPTER 4

The New Model of Relationship

It's true that it's a long jump from the old model of relationship to the new one. But what the last chapter said about cycles still holds true in this one: Once we grab onto part of a cycle, it tends to start pulling us in. Even if we can try only a few parts of the new model now, it will help. And as we start to feel some improvement in our relationships, we can get the courage to try more.

Of course, when we talk about the "old" and "new" models, we know that those terms aren't absolute. There will always be people who relate in the clumsy and cruel ways described in the old model. And there have always been people who treated one another with the love, friendship, and respect that run the new model.

But the words "old" and "new" are important in describing where each model sits in the development of the human race—and the development of an individual life. The old model gets its power from the primitive, incomplete understanding of a small child or a prehistoric human being. The new model gets its power from some of the higher ideals and values that people and cultures have been trying so hard to live by.

It's a funny thing about higher ideals and values: We don't have to be sure about them, or even understand them, in order to have them. Whenever we act on them, we have them. Whenever we act against them, we lose sight of them for a while—no matter how good we are at talking about them. Our development as people rides forward and backward on our willingness to try to do the right thing, even when we're not sure what that is.

> **All relationships have some pain. It's our reactions to pain—our fear-based beliefs, thoughts, feelings, and actions—that cause problems.**

The other strange thing about higher ideals and values is that they work. These kinds of ideals have popped up in just about every century and culture, among people who have dedicated their lives to finding out what's good and true. But the reason they've pointed to certain values is not because those values are "holy" and hard to live up to. It's because, when we act on those ideals and values, things go much more smoothly.

The world was probably meant to run more smoothly than it's been running. So are people. So are relationships—even dating relationships. There will always be pain. But it's our reactions to pain—our fear-based beliefs, thoughts, feelings, and actions—that cause destructive cycles like the old model. That's where we lose our balance, dignity, and respect for one another.

Here's a point-by-point description of the new model of relationship. Its five phases are: (1) dignity, (2) beliefs based on love, (3) whole thinking, (4) friendship, and (5) respect. Please compare it with the old model—and with your own experience—and grab on wherever you can.

Phase One: Dignity

To understand dignity we usually have to erase most of the things we learned about the word when we were children. Dignity doesn't mean having our hair combed and wearing a dress or suit. It doesn't mean being stiff and formal, or raising our eyebrows when other people make mistakes. It doesn't mean we don't make mistakes, either. And it certainly doesn't mean that we're better than anyone else. It just means we're worthy and whole.

When we're dignified, we're in balance. We know our own worth, being deeply rooted in an honest knowledge of who we are. Things that happen to us might make us happy or sad. They might hurt us deeply. But they don't make us lose our sense of balance, our sense of peace, or knowledge of our own worth. We don't lose our feeling of being whole. We don't turn against ourselves.

> **When we're dignified, we're in balance. We know our own worth.**

If dignity is the opposite of humiliation, then how do dignified people react to the experience of pain, shame, and powerlessness? They don't strike out at others, because that would destroy their balance and their peace. They don't cave in and decide they're worthless, because that would do the same thing. Instead, they choose a third reaction: humility. Humility makes us flexible, and something that's flexible is much less likely to be broken than something that can't bend.

If the most common reaction to humiliation is an escape into fear, what's the most common reaction to dignity? Dignity holds us in place. It doesn't toss us around like humiliation does. So our most common reaction to dignity is simply to live our lives. We just follow our true nature. Many say that our true nature as human beings leads us to love other people. So the second phase of the new model is called "beliefs based on love."

Phase Two: Beliefs Based on Love

The love that drives these beliefs isn't what the popular culture calls love. It isn't that feeling that makes us long for someone special—who just *has* to love us the same way in return or we'll die. In fact, love isn't a feeling at all. It's a decision. In *The Road Less Traveled*, M. Scott Peck defined love as "The will to extend one's self for the purpose of nurturing one's own or another's spiritual growth." In love, we're committed to our own well-being and to the well-being of others.

By this definition, love doesn't make us stop taking care of ourselves. It doesn't throw us off balance like the emotions we've been taught to call love. And it definitely doesn't make us spend time with people who are dangerous to us. It just gives us a solid foundation for a set of beliefs. Those beliefs can lead us back into dignity and forward into happy and peaceful experiences.

Here are the beliefs that are the opposites of the fear-based beliefs described in the last chapter:

1. *I'm complete.* I'm a whole person. I may need people and things, but I don't need them to complete me. I have nothing to prove. Even if I've been injured in my life, I also know I'm capable of healing. I'm at peace.

2. *There's plenty to go around.* There are plenty of men, women, and partners around, and I'll meet quite a few of them. I don't have to worry about which of my wants or needs will be filled. I can relax. It's okay to want a romantic relationship or a sexual partner. But if a partner is what I really need, the right one will probably be attracted to me at the right time. I don't have to lie to myself or try to force this one to be "the one."

3. *I matter*. Within this relationship, with this person, what I do and don't want really matters. I have a right to have desires and a right to tell the other person about them. The other person has a right to refuse if his or her desires don't match mine. I have a right to set limits and make sure no one crosses those lines. I deserve to be treated with respect and so does the other person.

4. *I need to be honest with myself.* My relationship with the truth is one of the most important relationships I'll ever have. If I ignore what I see or hear—or what my "gut" tells me—I'll betray myself. I owe it to myself, and to others, to be honest with myself.

5. *We're all in this together*. Men and women may have some different experiences, but we're all the same at heart. We all started out as innocent children, and we're doing the best we can to survive and make sense of our lives. Women and men both feel powerless sometimes. That's one of the things that makes us act so crazy. Even if this person *thinks* I'm his or her enemy, that doesn't *make* him or her my enemy. Sometimes the most loving thing I can do is to get out of the situation. But I can do that without turning this person into a monster in my head.

6. *I'm a choice maker*. I have the right to choose the kind of life that's good for me. I'm not to blame for the things other people have done to me, but I am responsible for my own actions. I'm not responsible for taking care of this person's feelings, but I am responsible for taking care of myself. I have many options to choose from and the power to choose.

Beliefs Based on Love
1. I'm complete.
2. There's plenty to go around.
3. I matter.
4. I need to be honest with myself.
5. We're all in this together.
6. I'm a choice maker.

This set of beliefs would probably seem quite foreign to our friends Don and Sandy. In some ways they've been caught up in everyone else's beliefs all their lives. If they wanted to try on a more peaceful set, they'd probably have to do some work.

The old beliefs that run our lives are often called "old tapes." These are messages we've heard over and over until we repeat them to ourselves without thinking. One of the best ways to deal with these old tapes is to tape over them. The first step is to notice the old tapes as they play in our heads and admit that we're just thinking thoughts that someone else planted there. Then we choose the new beliefs that will lead us toward better experiences. We start repeating these new beliefs to ourselves over and over. That was how we learned the old beliefs—by hearing them repeated to us all our lives. One place to start might be by memorizing some of the beliefs listed above and repeating them when we need them.

It feels silly at first, but after a while it becomes easier and more automatic. In time we find ourselves believing new things and thinking in new ways that feel a lot better than the old ways. That leads us to the next phase: whole thinking.

Phase Three: Whole Thinking

This phase is called "whole thinking" because it's based on reality as a whole, and on the belief that we're whole people. These six ways of thinking follow from the beliefs listed under the last phase. They're the opposites of the kinds of "broken thinking" listed in the last chapter.

1. *Seeing people as people.* If I don't need other people to complete me, then I can just let them be whoever they are. They don't need to fulfill my need for sex, love, commitment, revenge, healing, or anything else. I can value people highly even if I can't "use" them.

2. *Faith and patience.* I believe that there's enough and that I'll get what I really need when the time is right. And so I don't have to put any pressure on this person, this date, this relationship, to be anything but what they naturally turn out to be. I don't have to see people of my own sex as competition. We can *all* get what we need, and we can help one another in the process.

3. *Clear self-knowledge.* If what I want or don't want really matters, then it's my job to figure out what that is. I'm the only one who can do that. I search my mind, heart, gut instinct, and feelings of desire (or no desire). I weigh all the information they give me. I take the time needed to figure out my real wants, needs, and expectations. Then I make decisions about any desires that I might want to talk about, or limits that I might want to set.

4. *Attention to my reality.* I look at the situation—the person, what's happening, and my feelings about it—as it really is. I don't let myself be distracted by the way I'd like things to be, or the way I've been taught they should be. I look for the truth, no more and no less. Sometimes my gut instinct works much better than my logic, so I pay special attention to it. If it tells me something's wrong, I take immediate steps to be safe—no matter what my brain says.

5. *Compassion.* If we're all in this together, then I look at this person as a brother or a sister. I look at myself the same way. My first priority is the well-being of each one of us. I don't want to force anything, and I won't let myself be forced. I'd like this time together to leave both of us a little better off. I'd like each of us to remember the other as someone who supported the personal and spiritual growth of both people.

6. *Awareness of choices.* If I believe I'm a choice maker, then I get down to the business of finding out what my true feelings and options are. I use my logic, my imagination, and my instincts. I use everything I've heard or read on the subject. I put them all together and think of all the choices I have. It's never just one or two. I don't rule out any options too quickly. *But I don't let anyone else make my choices for me.*

Beliefs Based on Love	Whole Thinking
1. I'm complete.	Seeing people as people
2. There's plenty to go around	Faith and patience
3. I matter.	Clear self-knowledge
4. I need to be honest with myself.	Attention to reality
5. We're all in this together.	Compassion
6. I'm a choice maker.	Awareness of choices

Like the beliefs described in phase one of the new model, these ways of thinking might be new to Don and Sandy. Taking on new thought patterns is like any other skill. It starts with the willingness to try, to practice over and over, and to forgive ourselves when we make mistakes.

Unless we work on beliefs and thought patterns, it's almost impossible to change the way we feel, act, and react. And if we don't change our actions, we're almost sure to get more of the same pain—sooner or later. The next phase, friendship, shows what can happen when we learn the art of whole thinking.

Phase Four: Friendship

This phase takes its title from the most important goal of any relationship: friendship. Sex might satisfy some desires, but if it comes without friendship, it leaves us lonelier than we started A committed relationship might bring feelings of security, but a committed relationship without friendship is much worse than no relationship at all.

In the new model, friendship takes its place opposite the "panic and power games" phase of the old model. That phase was driven by fear, while friendship gets its strength from love. Of course, the actions described below aren't the only ways of being a friend. But they're a good start.

1. *Letting things unfold.* When I feel complete, I can give up the need to try to control people and situations. I have the luxury of being myself and letting things happen naturally. I can want things to happen without feeling as if I need to have them happen. That doesn't mean I don't say what I want or stand up for my limits. But it does mean I don't feel like I have to lie or try to impress anyone.

2. *Going slowly.* Now that I know my true needs will be filled at the right time, I have no need to rush things. I know that safety is only one of the benefits of taking a relationship slowly and carefully. The other benefits are many. We actually have a chance of forming a true friendship. I can take the time I need to figure out what I really want. I can look at the relationship honestly to see if it's healthy. If this relationship fits any of the patterns that have caused me problems before, I can take steps to make sure I'm safe. I can also start thinking about what those patterns might be saying about me and my relationships.

3. *Clear and honest communication.* When I've taken the time to find out what my true wants, limits, and expectations are, I make sure the other person knows about them. There are many ways of doing this. I choose ways that are honest, respectful, and friendly. I listen and pay attention to what the other person says in return. If I realize I've been sending double messages, I correct the problem immediately. If we both choose nonverbal ways of communicating, I make sure my message is clearly understood. If that doesn't work, I switch to words. I do all I can to make sure we understand one another.

4. *Being careful.* I act on my gut feelings and my honest view of the situation. If I feel safe, I still take things slowly and carefully, for the sake of the friendship. But if I feel I'm in any danger with this person, I make sure I'm not alone with him or her at all—not even in a car. If I'm a woman, I don't go to any parties unless I'm sure they're safe. If I feel something's getting strange, I get out. If I can get out gracefully, I do. If not, I still get out. I don't worry about being embarrassed or embarrassing my date. I can always deal with embarrassment later. The most important thing is staying safe.

5. *Shared power.* I've decided we're all in this together, and I've made a commitment to the well-being of both of us. Now I act on that commitment by treating this person with consistent respect. If I have power, I don't abuse it. If the other person denies his or her power, I try to help him or her find it. As long as I help this person become more powerful, I become more powerful. If he or she tries to deny or take away my power, I set clear limits. If that doesn't work, I get out of the situation. I know that giving up my power won't help either of us.

6. *Freedom.* I've defined myself as a choice maker and I've become aware of all my options. Now it's time to make the best choices I can. I know I'll make mistakes. That's part of being alive. I know many of my choices will have some consequences I don't like. But if I do my best to make honest, careful, and respectful choices, I'll be able to handle the consequences. I'm willing to take responsibility for the effects of my actions. I'm willing to act as a free, responsible human being and to treat others as the same.

Beliefs Based on Love	Whole Thinking	Friendship
1. I'm complete.	Seeing people as people	Letting things unfold
2. There's plenty to go around.	Faith and patience	Going slowly
3. I matter.	Clear self-knowledge	Clear and honest communication.
4. I need to be honest with myself.	Attention to reality	Being careful
5. We're all in this together.	Compassion	Shared power
6. I'm a choice maker.	Awareness of choices	Freedom

The way Don and Sandy were headed in chapter two, they'll probably never get to this point—at least, not with each other and not tonight. Friendship as it has been described here is the last thing on Don's mind, and Sandy hasn't searched her own mind far enough to know what she wants.

If these skills seem difficult, remember that they're backed up with changed beliefs and thinking patterns. If we take it step by step, it's much easier. And when we act out of friendship, it prepares us to move to the final phase: respect.

Phase Five: Respect

Respect is closely related to dignity, but it's different. Dignity is something we *have*. Respect is something we *do*—to

79

ourselves and to others. We show by our thoughts, words, and actions that we consider each person worthy. Respect is based on dignity and leads to more dignity. It's important to both men and women.

If we don't respect ourselves, it's hard to respect others. We might obey them or try to please them, but that's not the same thing. And if we don't treat others with respect, it's hard to treat ourselves with respect. We might think we respect ourselves, but it usually rings hollow.

It's also difficult to impossible to respect ourselves or others when we're being driven by fear. When we panic, we get clumsy. When we start playing power games, we throw respect out the window. When we forget about friendship, we forget about respect.

Respect isn't empty of sexual feelings and desires. It's not the opposite of passion. In fact, respect can make passion run deeper because it carries us closer to the humanity of the people we desire. It leads us to real intimacy. Just taking the passion out of something won't make it respectful. And having sex with someone we don't desire is definitely not respectful—to ourselves or to the other person.

> **Respect can make passion run deeper, because it carries us closer to the humanity of the people we desire. It leads us to real intimacy.**

Respect shows up in many forms. It might take the form of a couple's decision to call it an evening, because they've talked and realized that their expectations don't match. They might decide to try again another day, or they might decide to wait for people whose desires match their own. For the couple whose desires match, respect might take the form of a decision to set—and follow—clear limits on what will and won'thappen.

If one partner is trying to manipulate another into saying yes, respect might take the form of a polite but definite refusal. The partner who refuses isn't losing his or her temper, but he or she makes it clear that the manipulation isn't going to work. And for the partner who wants to manipulate, respect takes the form of a decision not to even try it.

For a woman who senses danger in a man, respect usually takes the form of a quick exit—with or without appropriate excuses—before she's left alone with the danger. She often doesn't explain it to him at the time, because that might increase the danger. At this point her only responsibility is to be safe.

For a man who has had the urge to rape, respect will lead him to get professional help as soon as possible. It will also lead him to avoid being alone with women until he's received that help—and found his beliefs, thought patterns, feelings, and actions changing. For a woman who has a history of being manipulated or raped, respect will also lead her to get professional help.

In all these cases, respect also leads back to dignity. Each person does what it takes to be honest and responsible, and to take care of him- or herself. From dignity we set off again on this circle of healing. It's as if the old model is a downward spiral—covering the same ground, but digging us deeper and deeper. The new model is an upward spiral, always taking us to higher ground.

Please believe this: It's where we all belong.

Journal Questions

1. How have you been taught to define dignity? How do you feel about the idea of dignity? What kinds of actions or situations can make you feel as if you have dignity?

2. What's your definition of love? Where did you learn that definition? What do you think of the definition listed in this chapter?

3. How many of the items listed under "whole thinking" do you find yourself doing when you're with—or thinking about—people you're dating or considering dating?

4. Were you one of the many who were raised to think that friendship has to be nonsexual? Have you ever known any couples who had true friendship and had truly sexual relationships together?

5. The authors talk about the need to respect others in order to respect yourselves, and vice versa. Does this make sense to you? Can you think of any incidents in your life that might support this idea?

PART III

How We
Got Here

CHAPTER 5

Our Legacy

The past doesn't create the future, but the past is with us, always pushing us in one direction or another. It's helpful to know which beliefs and thoughts are really our own and which ones we simply inherited from our history as men and women, our cultures, or our early training.

This chapter looks at:

- how our brains sometimes add to the risk of sexual aggression

- how our history taught us to see one another as commodities

- how we still hear some of those old messages from our history

---

Many of men's and women's attitudes toward one another aren't freely chosen. In many ways we've been set up to see one another as enemies. The next two chapters will look at the "setup factors" in the cultures and communities where we're raised, then zero in on children's experiences in their families. But first, this chapter looks at some of the effects of human biology and history on men's and women's attitudes toward one another.

Evolution and the Brain

It might seem like a simple task: As time passes, the human race just evolves. We learn new things about what works and what doesn't—and what hurts and what doesn't. We replace our old ways of doing things. But over the centuries, as human beings have grown more civilized, we've also kept many of our old, less civilized ways. There are psychological reasons for this—superstition, selfishness, fear of changing—but there are biological reasons, too.

Each of us has three brains. As a species we developed these brains one by one as we evolved. The new ones didn't just replace the old ones. They wrapped around them in layers. All three brains have important functions.

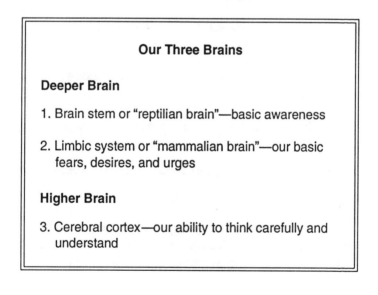

Our Three Brains

Deeper Brain

1. Brain stem or "reptilian brain"—basic awareness

2. Limbic system or "mammalian brain"—our basic fears, desires, and urges

Higher Brain

3. Cerebral cortex—our ability to think carefully and understand

The Deeper Brain

The first two brains are sometimes thought of together as the "deeper brain." They're located at the center or base of the brain. They're in charge of our primitive functions—basic survival, desires, and emotions.

The **brain stem,** or "reptilian brain," developed millions of years ago, before we even crawled out of the water. This is the center that controls whether or not we're awake and alert. The brain stem works closely with the second brain, the limbic system.

The **limbic system** is sometimes called the "mammalian brain" because it developed when we became mammals—still quite a long time ago. This is the part of the brain that tells us to form families and communities. It's also the part that tells us to start wars, hold onto old hurts, and get revenge.

When we feel threatened our bodies are filled with chemicals that speed up our heart rate and breathing. At the same time, the deeper brain is filled with chemicals that tell us to fight, run away, or "freeze." As a result, we feel scared and/or angry. If we just listen to the deeper brain, we'll probably react by getting violent—or panicking and not being able to protect ourselves.

Feelings of love, sexual desire, and physical hunger also take the form of chemical messages through the deeper structures of the brain. We might feel these as, for example, a desire to hug someone, to do something sexual, or to eat. If there's a good reason not to act on these desires, the deeper brain won't understand. It just wants what it wants—when it wants it.

The Higher Brain

The **cerebral cortex,** or "higher brain," came with our evolution into human form. This is where we try to understand it all—ourselves, other people, the world—why we're here and what it all means. This is the brain that forms value systems and thinks about right and wrong.

This is the brain that can rise above old resentments and forgive someone we thought was our enemy. It's also the brain that can think up complicated schemes to use, hurt, rape, or kill people. The cerebral cortex was designed to balance all three brains—not to shut off the other two, but to harmonize them. This is the brain that can let us have both passion and safety.

The Whole Brain

These three brains work together well. But at any time, any one of them can drown the others out. If we choose to, we can train the higher brain to learn, understand, and help us try to do the right thing. But without warning, a number of things can throw us back into our deeper, more primitive brain.

Fear and anger can set off those primitive functions. The same is true for hunger, emotional stress, being tired, or having sexual desire. So can alcohol and other drugs, and the effects of addiction. When that happens, the feelings of fear and need in the deeper brain will tell the higher brain where to aim its powers. We might react by using our higher brain to help us manipulate another person.

Anger and fear also can lead to something called **flooding**. Flooding is a state where our brain chemicals put our deeper brains in "overdrive" and keep us from hearing what our higher brains are saying. If we're angry, we might not be able to think of any choices besides violence. If we're afraid, we might freeze and not be able to defend ourselves. That's why some rape victims don't escape or fight back. Their brains are flooded with powerful chemicals and they can't think clearly.

> **We get into trouble when:**
>
> - fear, anger, stress, desire, or substances trigger our deeper brain and we can't think clearly or don't control our actions
>
>   or
>
> - we ignore the danger signals from our deeper brain and try to explain them away with our higher brain

At other times we can count too much on the higher brain and block out important signals from the deeper brain. If someone shows subtle signs of being dangerous, the higher brain might not notice. It might be too busy with all our plans and expectations for this person. But the lower brain—our survival system—might notice the danger. We might have a strange feeling near the pit of the stomach or a doubt that we don't understand. If the higher brain ignores or denies those feelings, we're in trouble.

Brain Chemicals

Our thoughts and urges can be traced to the chemicals that travel through the body and brain. For example, people who have too little of a brain chemical called "serotonin" tend to have a hard time resisting some of the basic, deeper-brain urges—like the urge to be violent, to act sexually, or to eat too much. Alcohol and other drugs lower the level of serotonin in our brains. But there are certain foods, vitamins, and prescription drugs that can raise serotonin levels.

There's also a chemical called "noradrenaline" that pumps up our feelings of fear and anger. This is the chemical that fills the brain in flooding. People who have too much norad-renaline have a hard time not being violent. But some people seem to have "used up" all their noradrenaline. They have difficulty feeling anything. High levels of noradrenaline can lead to impulsive, "hot-blooded" violence, but low levels can lead to careful, "cold-blooded" violence. Alcohol and other drugs also raise our level of noradrenaline.

Scientists now believe that growing up in violent homes or communities can change our brain chemistry. It can set our serotonin levels too low or our noradrenaline levels too high. It can lead to many problems that make us more likely to be violent or less likely to protect ourselves. Children don't choose to be born or raised in violent settings. It's sad to hear that some of the effects can make it harder to avoid more violence later in life.

Do We Have any Choice?

We may still be wired for primitive urges and reactions, but we also have what we need to understand and make careful choices. The way our brains and brain chemicals are set up doesn't mean we have to choose violence or manipulation. But it does mean that our highest motives have some pretty stiff competition. It's true that we're an amazing, highly evolved species. But we're also everything else we've ever been.

The Evolution of Gender Roles

Like the brain, the rest of the body also has a history. If our roles as women and men are a little confusing, it helps if we trace them back to their beginnings. We can see how different the circumstances were when men and women first took on their old roles—roles that still get us in trouble, no matter how much we appear to have changed.

As sexual beings, we're really pretty simple: Our sexual functions were designed to keep the species going. That meant that, when we first became human, the woman's job was to have children and keep them alive. The man's job was to get her pregnant and help her protect the children. In those primitive times, our sexual desires and our attitudes toward potential partners were all aimed toward that goal.

When our roles as men and women were being developed, we didn't have the skills to question what we did. We just did what seemed necessary to survive.

That was before we learned how to use our higher brains. It was before we figured out that having child after child was hard on a woman's body, mind, and emotions—or before we realized that those things mattered. It was before we had birth control or careers, and before societies even considered love a good reason for choosing a mate. We didn't have the skills then to question and debate what we did. We just did it.

The Beginning of Commodity Thinking

It was in those times that men and women began to think of one another as commodities. It was the woman's job to raise the strongest children she could. Living conditions were so rough that, even with the best care, large numbers of children died.

It made sense for a woman to look for the strongest, most potent, and most fertile man—one who could father many children, pass on good genes, and be willing and able to protect her and her children. A woman's sexual attractiveness was a tool for attracting men. The better she was at attracting them, the more men she had to choose from.

One of the man's jobs was to prove how well he could father children. He could do this by having sex with a number of women. When a man developed family instincts, he looked for a woman who could arouse him sexually and have many children. But his instincts would lead him only to protect and feed his own children. To make sure all the children were his own, it made sense for him to choose a woman who hadn't had sex with any other men.

A man's other job was to prove what a good protector he was. As civilizations began to fight for control of land and human lives, men became the warriors. Their bodies became weapons for taking and keeping power. They were asked to kill people they did or didn't know, and to die trying to defend power that was beyond their control. Above all, they were asked to win, no matter what it took.

Commodity Thinking in the Cave Days

A woman's job was to:
- raise the strongest children she could
- attract a man who could father and protect her children
- prove that the children were fathered by her mate

A man's job was to:
- prove that he could father children
- prove that he was a good provider and protector
- be willing to fight and die in battle

Each gender took on the role of a commodity for the other.

So the commodity thinking began, and with it came conflict. A woman's sexuality was a commodity for attracting a man's desire, but her virginity was a commodity for attracting his protection. That was when she first took responsibility for refusing—or trying to refuse—sex. It was necessary for her own survival and for the survival of her children. A woman's ability to have children was a commodity for the community's survival. But the act of having child after child weakened her health and raised her risk of dying in childbirth.

A man's ability to father children was a commodity for winning a mate, but that ability could be proven only by the "conquest" of women. A man's body—his ability to fight and kill, and his willingness to be killed in battle—was another commodity that decided his value to the culture. His body was also a commodity for winning a mate. But the stronger he was, the easier it was for him to use that strength against a woman. And his whole social training as a warrior had been designed to convince him that "might makes right."

Children were considered commodities, too. Boys could be trained to hunt, fight, or gather food, and girls could grow up to make more children and keep the species going. But as some civilizations grew, the need for more food and land grew greater than the need for more people. These civilizations began to see female children as less valuable than male children. After all, their primary function in life would be to make more people, rather than to help feed them. Women were smaller and physically weaker than men, and pregnancy and child care often used up all their strength.

The Growth of Civilizations

If you've ever listened to a developing child, you've probably heard a long string of attempts to explain and control the world. Those attempts start out very primitive—even silly—

then get more and more reasonable as the child grows up. In time the child learns that Mommy doesn't just disappear. She goes to the store, but she always comes back. Even so, rational adults sometimes find themselves caught up in fears that they know don't make sense—like the fear of being abandoned. Those fears usually started in childhood. Even though their changing views of reality covered the old fears up, they didn't get rid of them.

> **Old beliefs and practices don't always disappear. Often they just go underground. People deny them but still act as if the old rules were in place.**

Civilizations often develop the same way. Each culture forms laws, rituals, and institutions around the things it holds most important. These customs often change as the civilizations "grow up." But even so, pieces of the old ways remain. Old beliefs and practices don't always disappear. Often they just go underground. People deny them but still act as if the old rules were in place.

The result is confusion. The old messages are distorted but they're still communicated. In times of stress, the conflict between those two voices can be deafening. The past no longer works, but it has the power to hurt the present and the future. That's where we are now with women's and men's roles, and the way we relate to one another.

Myths About Women's Sexuality

Many cultures developed whole systems of mythology that supported the claim that women were created to bear children and obey men. Because they had the ability to carry life, women were thought to be tied to the natural world—the world of plants, animals, and the earth. Men were thought to be more closely connected with the supernatural—God or the spirit world. In Western cultures, the natural world was thought of as separate from, inferior to, and even at war with the supernatural.

For this reason, women were sometimes considered "temptresses." Their sexuality was thought of as both powerful and forbidden. While most cultures took men's sexual desires for granted, many began to look down on women's desires—or to believe that desire was unnatural for women. A woman learned to be ashamed if she desired a man—or if she didn't desire the man her family wanted her to marry. She also learned to blame herself if a man took her by force.

Myths About Men's Roles

The cultures that went to war also developed myths to explain the use of men as weapons. Whoever a culture's god(s) might be, they had decided that this culture was supposed to win over the other cultures. So it was okay for men to kill and be killed defending that "right."

What's Wrong with This Picture?

Women's main role was supposed to be to have sex and children, but their sexuality was often thought of as forbidden and shameful.

Men were trained to fight and kill in wars, then expected to come home and be peaceful and loving with their families.

95

Of course, when and if these "killing machines" came home, they were expected to magically turn into gentle, loving, socially acceptable husbands and fathers. But they were still supposed to be able to kill or be killed at the drop of a hat to defend their families and communities. The ideal for a man was to be a socially acceptable killer.

Old and New Messages

As basic survival became easier, people began to develop their higher brain functions—for both selfish and unselfish purposes. They learned better and better ways of protecting people—and worse and worse ways of abusing them. This abuse of power was hardest on people who were weaker in terms of money, physical strength, or freedom. Women, children, slaves, and people with illnesses or disabilities often suffered.

Civilizations and cultures developed to help people try to understand, survive—and in some cases, exploit—an increasingly complicated world. The old, primitive messages weren't destroyed or "taped over." They were blended in with the new messages. They made an uneven, confusing, troubling place for a child to be born.

As the earlier chapters have shown, the echoes of the old messages affect many areas of our lives today. Children hear them in the things their family members say, in the way the adults in their lives treat one another, and in the many "rules" their friends explain to them. Boys and girls are still learning different sets of rules, as if they're still being set up for conflict. It's not too hard to see how these rules evolved from cave times.

Our new roles for women and men haven't made all the changes some hoped they'd make. For many people it's still about "who wants what from whom." With all these expectations, the possibility of friendship can fall by the wayside. Many boys are still being taught to look for girls who'll "put out," and many girls are taught to look for a "good catch." On some levels, nothing has changed since the species began.

Just as our lower and higher brains share the same head, so do our earliest and latest cultural memories. We keep growing more sophisticated, but we're still being taught to look at people as commodities. We may be reaching for the stars, but we're dragging our past behind us.

Building a Different Future

Many of the old cultural traditions are beautiful and should never be threatened or replaced. They should be given a place of honor and used to weave new traditions. Others, like the sex and gender attitudes described above, are destructive. They no longer fit the species as it has evolved. But in American society, where everything is advertised as "new and different," we tend to underestimate the effects of the past on the present. That puts the future at risk.

> **Each of us has a choice—the choice to learn, understand, and practice new ways of doing things. We can rise above our history.**

As a culture we're proud of saying we want fairness, equal opportunity, and well-being for all people. But if we really want all these things, first we need to identify all the obstacles inside our own minds. We need to understand and admit the influence history has on us, even if it makes us look less self-determined than we wanted to be. Only by admitting where we really are can we take the first step toward where we want to be.

Scientists say even the smartest people use only 10 percent of their brains. Most of us use 5 percent or less. That means that, as a species, we have a lot farther to go in our evolution. No one knows for sure what will happen. We might mess it all up with fear, selfishness, and conflict. Or we might rise above all that.

But each one of us—each woman, each man—has a choice. Right now, on this knife blade between the past and the future, we can choose to learn. We can choose to understand and practice new ways of doing things. We can choose to rise above.

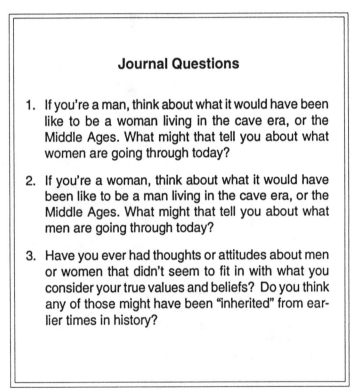

Journal Questions

1. If you're a man, think about what it would have been like to be a woman living in the cave era, or the Middle Ages. What might that tell you about what women are going through today?

2. If you're a woman, think about what it would have been like to be a man living in the cave era, or the Middle Ages. What might that tell you about what men are going through today?

3. Have you ever had thoughts or attitudes about men or women that didn't seem to fit in with what you consider your true values and beliefs? Do you think any of those might have been "inherited" from earlier times in history?

CHAPTER 6

The Commodity Culture

It's no wonder so many of us buy into the old-model idea that people are things to be used. It's one of the strongest messages we get from our popular culture. But believe it or not, the culture is our servant, not our master. We make it, and enough of us working together can change important parts of it.

In America, pop-culture-bashing is a popular sport. The culture gets much of the blame for violence in the community, abuse in the home, illiteracy, the loss of moral values, and most of the other problems we face. As broad, brassy, powerful, and crazy as it is, this culture makes a tempting target. Much of what you read in this chapter will sound familiar and probably ring true.

This chapter looks at:

- how women are "sold" as commodities
- men as commodities for security, power, and protection
- what real men and women might be
- what power really means

It's hard to say how the blending of hundreds of cultures in this country brought us to the huge bundle of contradictions we wake up to today. As a culture, we're like a puppy whose feet are too big. We're rich and poor, soft-hearted and selfish, a con artist who's easily tricked. Other cultures see us as completely caught up in buying and selling, spending and getting things. They're not far from the truth.

Survival seems to be the main thing, as it was for the men and women in the cave days. To many people, making a profit seems to be the easiest way to survive, so many people have learned how to do just that. The industries that make the largest profits have the most power—including the power to tell us what to eat, think, drive, drink, wear, want, watch on TV, believe, and do on our days off.

As a culture we're fiercely proud of our ability to think for ourselves. But with all those messages coming at us from all directions, how can we really tell which thoughts are our own?

The old, primitive messages about women and men as commodities haven't just been whispered to us through the ages. They've been shot up in lights in Las Vegas. We have a double whammy. We have the old superstitions dropped down through our cultures of origin. But we also have new messages in surround-sound, telling us that women and men are commodities, and that sex and violence go together.

Women as Commodities

In television and movies, women as commodities are taken for granted. Women's sexuality is glorified, but it's also often shown as something dangerous or dirty. A woman's "attractiveness" is almost always taken to mean her sexual attractiveness—and that's almost always taken to mean her physical appearance. Most "love" stories focus on the process of "getting" the loved one, for sex and/or marriage. It's as if whatever happens after that doesn't matter.

Sex and violence are paired so often that many people learn to think and speak of them together. A female character's vulnerability to attack is considered a definite "turn-on." Another favorite sex object is the ruthless, selfish woman who uses her sexuality to get what she wants. This feeds straight into the belief that men have to use whatever weapons they have in this battle of the sexes.

Women as Commodities in the Media

- Women's sexuality is glorified, but also shown as dangerous or dirty.
- A woman's vulnerability to attack is considered a "turn on."
- Physical beauty and sexuality are used to buy men's attention.

In prime time, children sit in front of the tube and watch scenes of seduction, manipulation, exploitation, rape, emotional abuse, bitter conflict, beatings, and murder. For every example of the new model of relationship on TV, children see many, many more examples of the old model. Often there's no adult around who can help them understand what they're watching—or help them turn it off.

The fashion and "beauty" industries bring women's commodity value home. They encourage women to starve themselves, ruin their skin with makeup, ruin their feet and backs with high heels, and ruin their credit lines with clothes and jewelry. The not-so-well-hidden message in all this is that physical beauty—as the culture defines it—is the currency that women use to buy men's attention.[1]

Prostitution and pornography just take that process one step further by making the sexual part explicit. It's sex for sale, no more and no less. But how different is that, really, from selling beauty or sexual vulnerability?

The Economics of Being Female

It almost sounds silly to say that many women still believe they have to "get" a man. Aren't most women more independent? Don't women play an important part in the workplace? Yes to both questions—but inequalities still exist, and double messages still get communicated.

It's true that fewer women feel a need for a man's financial support. But even successful, independent women sometimes find themselves looking for love and commitment in relationships where the men turn out to be looking for desire and convenience—and nothing more.

Connie is one example. At the age of thirty-four Connie has made more friends, more money, and more good contacts than most people make in a lifetime. But she keeps getting into painful, old-model relationships with the same kind of man. He's never capable of giving her the commitment she wants, but each time she tells herself he's different from the others. And in many ways, of course, he is. But in a few key areas, he's very much like the rest of the men she's dated.

For women like Connie this search for committed love is more than the simple, healthy desire to love and form a partnership with another. Repeated mistakes aren't caused by desire. They're caused by desperation. Connie's search is the search for a commodity, one she's been taught she has to get.

For many women, finance plays into it, too. Opportunities for women are improving in many ways. But many women are still being raised to believe that they don't deserve—or don't have access to—those opportunities. They learn that from subtle and not-so-subtle messages from families, friends, boyfriends, neighbors, and the media.

Some women face obstacles that are very real and almost impossible to overcome. Karen is a young mother who depends on welfare for her three children's survival. If she gets a job she'll lose all her benefits, including her housing supplement and health care for her children. She hasn't had time to build the skills that would earn her a good salary and benefit package. And every time she turns on the TV or radio—or listens to her relatives—she hears the message that what she needs is a good man. For some women, the drive to find a man might mean a jump to a higher level of status and security. But for others, it feels like the only way out of poverty and hopelessness.

> **Many women who have a lot going for them have been convinced that they need a man, and that there aren't enough to go around. They feel desperate.**

And for many women, the urge to find a man is one they don't completely understand. Maybe they really want satisfying sex. Maybe they really want friendship and companionship. Maybe they really want children. But all their lives they've been told—in many voices—that they need a man. They've also been told there aren't enough good men to go around. They've been programmed to feel desperate and to feel competitive with other women.

This would just be an annoying and frustrating problem, but some women's experiences make it serious—or even tragic. These include:

- women who ignore other aspects of their lives and put most of their energy into the search for a perfect man;
- women who can't have satisfying friendships with other women because they think of them as rivals;
- women who cancel their plans with female friends when a man calls for a last-minute date;
- women who are manipulated into having sex, which they believe will bring them closer to finding love;
- women who are raped in the dating ritual by men they trusted; and
- women who stay in abusive relationships because, for emotional or financial reasons, they fear being alone.

For these women, men are a commodity. But they're a dangerous, destructive commodity—and sometimes a deadly one.

Men as Commodities

Like many women, many men have been well programmed into their traditional roles. Unlike women, most men haven't spent the past three decades questioning and trying to reshape those roles. Men have been taught to think it "unmanly" even to question their roles as men. A man isn't supposed to question himself or ask for help. A man is supposed to "know."

Men as Commodities

- They are commodities for financial support.
- Their bodies are weapons of war.
- Their sexuality is a commodity for proving their manhood.

The men who have been exploring other options lately are finding it just as confusing as women have found it. Men are supposed to be the powerful ones, the ones in charge. But if you ask American men if they ever feel like commodities for other people's use, most will admit that they do.

Many men are still considered commodities for financial support and commodities for battle and protection. And after the loosening of sexual roles and rules in the seventies and eighties, many men also feel some pressure to be "studs." The image of the "sensitive man" has brought in one more challenge. Now the socially acceptable killing machine we met in the last chapter is also expected to give backrubs—and make tender, caring, passionate love for several hours at a moment's notice.

The popular culture's stable of standard male images has more variety than its collection of female images. But the male stereotypes are more intimidating to the ones who try to fulfill them:

- the tough, macho man-of-steel—all strength and no emotion
- the gorgeous stud, who charms and seduces one dazed woman after another
- the cold, calculating tycoon who builds an empire on raw nerve and ruthlessness
- the brilliant scientist, who doesn't understand women but has subatomic particles all figured out

There are many more, but you get the picture. All these stereotypes are rich and famous, driven and powerful. Their sexuality is almost always linked to their power. They prove that power by hurting or controlling other people—physically, psychologically, or financially.

Women are attracted to the power—possibly because they've denied their own power. So they put up with their partners' lack of compassion, and sometimes blame it on themselves. Some men are still being taught to be ashamed of their sensitivity and proud of being ruthless and heartless. They're expected to live through loss without grieving, and to survive violence without noticing their wounds or letting anyone help them.

Of course, if a man can't live up to one of these images, he can always be the lovable henpecked husband, the bungling clown, or the friendly neighborhood nerd. Many men—even ones who consider themselves "liberated"—have been trained to believe that mistakes would make them stupid, emotions would make them weak, vulnerability would leave them open to attack, and love and commitment would trap them and take away their freedom.

There's no room left for men to be what they really are: combinations of strength and weakness, pride and foolishness, emotion and fear of emotion, commitment and freedom. Men are trained to compare themselves with the ideal man on TV. In the face of that ideal, most men either develop illusions about who they really are, or decide that they're not good enough.

Men as Providers

Men have been taught to judge themselves on their value as providers, but:
- Blue-collar and middle-management positions have been cut drastically.
- Most families can't survive on one income.
- Divorced families struggle with divided incomes and attorneys' fees.
- Opportunities for men of color are often limited by discrimination.

Some men's feelings of fear and powerlessness turn to anger against women.

The Economics of Being Male

If women's sexuality has been turned into a commodity, so has men's financial success. Most men have been trained to judge themselves—and be judged—by their ability to earn a "good" living. But for many, the society that set up that standard can no longer give them the opportunity to earn even a moderate living.

Large sections of the job market, including blue-collar factory work and middle-management positions, have been cut as the industrial revolution has given way to the information age. Most families can't survive on one income. In many families where there are two adults, both work—or at least try to find work. Often these families are in worse financial shape than they would have been with one working adult in the 1960s.

And for the many families that divorce, things get a lot worse. Ending a marriage is painful. But it's made many times worse by the strain of trying to keep two households, raise children, and pay lawyers' fees on divided incomes.

Many people of color are hit the hardest by financial problems. In many African-American communities, prejudice, discrimination, and the lack of jobs combine to make work almost impossible to find. Many Latinos settle for subminimum wages—when they can find work—simply to survive.

Many men were raised to place their pride and self-worth on their power to earn and provide. For these men, the changing economy is a source of fear and frustration. They've been trained as commodities, but now they're being told that they're flawed. They feel worthless, powerless, and afraid.

Throughout history, a common reaction to feelings of powerlessness has been to find someone else who's even less powerful. Some men's feelings of fear and powerlessness lead them to feel angry at women and act in abusive ways. They might not notice the connection between those feelings and the things they do. The use of alcohol and other drugs often brings these problems to a head.

Violence toward women or children—physical, sexual, or emotional—might seem to take away the feelings of powerlessness for a little while. But violence always includes a loss of control. Later, looking back on that loss of control just makes the fear and sense of powerlessness stronger. If alcohol and drugs are a factor, more of these substances will be needed to dull the pain. The cycle of violence begins again.

Real Women, Real Men, Real Friendship

How do we get out of all this? How do we plug our ears to the popular culture's old-model messages? We can start by looking at our own values, beliefs, and thought patterns. We can ask ourselves: Is this what I choose, or has this been handed to me by my culture and its history? Is it working for me? Do I have other choices?

Real men and women are friends to themselves and to each other. They don't need to use one another. They don't need to play one-up or one-down.

Let's take the standard image of a woman. How important is physical beauty to attractiveness? Beauty fades so quickly, and the real interest is in a woman's thoughts, words, actions, and emotions. How can a woman's sexuality be "wrong" or "dirty" and still be a part of nature? Are sex and violence really linked, or is that just an illusion locked away in our deeper brains, left over from more primitive ages?

Does it make any sense for any woman today to feel as if her worth, success, and protection depend on finding the "right" man? Aren't there too many other ways of finding those things? And if she does choose to be in a relationship, won't it be better if she brings all those things in with her? Can it really be love if one partner feels trapped in the relationship by the need for money or security? Doesn't love have to be chosen freely?

And how about the standard image of a man? Isn't it time for more of us to admit that men are vulnerable and imperfect—and that's okay? Men can be wounded and traumatized, and they need to grieve and to heal. Men do feel uncertain and insecure some of the time. They need to ask for directions, or ask for help. They make mistakes. They're not all-powerful. It's all part of the job of being human. And being human is okay.

It's time to build a new vision for both men and women. We're all people who have strengths and weaknesses, who do things right and wrong. We're people who have grace and dignity and occasionally fall flat on our faces. Then we rise above it, and learn and grow from our mistakes.

Real women and men accept themselves as they are—with all the qualities they like about themselves, plus the qualities that get in the way. They try to know and respect the difference between the things they can and can't change. They learn when to fight for what they believe in, when to accept conditions they can't change, and when to leave.

Real men and women are friends to themselves, and to each other. They don't need to use one another. They don't need to play one-up or one-down. They don't act as if this is their last chance for sex, love, or marriage. They're willing to wait for the right time, the right people, and the right circumstances.

Real Power, True Worth

Most of the things we've been taught about power, and about men's and women's worth, are lies. Power isn't really measured by how much power we have over others. That's because there's always somebody who has more power over us. And eventually we die. If we play that game, it's just a question of when and how much we lose.

> **In the new model of relationship, true power isn't power over other people. It's power that we share with them.**

No matter how much of the old-model power we get, we're still letting someone else run our lives. We're letting the popular culture tell us what power is, what it does, and how to use it. Real power includes the ability to decide what power means to us.

In the new model of relationship, true power isn't power over other people. It's power that we share with them. It's the power to help others, and to accept their help. It's the power to stop doing things that hurt. It's the courage to be honest and open, to love and be loved. It's the courage to wait for what we need and accept ourselves and others exactly as we are. It's power over the illusions that are thrown at us every day.

There are also higher forms of power. People have different ways of looking at that. Some believe in a deity and call it by a name, like God, Allah, or the Great Spirit. Others see it as a form of energy that goes through everything. Many cultures have several deities. Some people just believe in their own ability to rise above their luck. And some simply believe in luck itself.

Our worth as human beings isn't really measured by money, beauty, brains, strength, or success. That's the same kind of game as power over others. If you're better than somebody, then you're also worse than somebody else. On that yardstick there's no such thing as good enough. Measuring ourselves against others is a recipe for insanity.

Some people believe that everyone is worthwhile just because we exist. Some of us have more luck, more money, more trouble, more teeth, and so on, but this doesn't raise or lower our value as people. If everyone is equal, people stop looking like commodities.

As long as we buy into that more-than/less-than thinking—even a little bit—we're vulnerable to every destructive message we hear. We'll be sizing ourselves up, and sizing up every potential partner we meet. And they'll be sizing us up, too.

As long as anybody can be bought and sold, nobody's free.

Notes

1. For a full discussion of this subject, see Naomi Wolf's *The Beauty Myth.*
2. Several books in the Bibliography address the attitudes that many women are taught concerning their needs or desires for men, love, and sex. Three examples would be Carol Cassell's Swept Away, Robin Norwood's *Women Who Love Too Much,* and Colette Dowling's *The Cinderella Complex.*

Journal Questions

1. In your own life, what part of the popular image of your gender have you found it hardest to live up to? What part has come easiest to you?

2. Have the images you mentioned in answering the previous question ever caused problems for you? For anyone you dated?

3. Describe an ideal image of a man or woman that doesn't make him or her a commodity, but just a free human being.

CHAPTER 7

Growing Up

Into this world—with its taking and using, its violent past and present—children are born. They're born vulnerable and sometimes amazingly strong.

We need to know how children

- learn about their value as human beings;
- learn to become women, men, and individuals;
- draw the boundaries around their lives; and
- experience abuse and trauma.

The adults who raise them were born vulnerable, too. Most of those adults have been knocked around—physically, sexually, and/or emotionally. Many have old scars, and some still have deep wounds that they don't know how to heal. Under this weight, though, they do the best they can to care for their children and raise them "the right way"—whatever that might be.

In their heads most parents hear all the old and new cultural messages about men and women. Whether or not they admit it, they're painfully aware of every place where they don't appear to measure up. Many still hear their parents' voices—

or their teachers' voices—telling them how bad, stupid, or limited they are. Sometimes these voices come out at their own children, as if the voices had a life of their own.

> **People aren't forced into destructive lifestyles by their past experiences. But it's much harder to swim against the current than with it.**

Many things that happen in childhood can make us more likely to follow the old model of relationship. They can also make us more likely to use sexual force and manipulation later in life, or more vulnerable to force and manipulation by others. Some of these set-up factors come from abuse, but others just come from things that can go wrong in ordinary childhood development.

Most children come through painful experiences with few lasting problems. They get the help they need wherever they can find it. They go on to live healthy, happy lives. Others get caught up in self-defeating, self-destructive patterns that they don't understand. Those patterns add more wounds to the unhealed places from childhood. People aren't forced into destructive lifestyles by their past experiences. But it's much harder to swim against the current than with it.

A few areas of childhood have strong effects on our ideas of relationship and on the way we relate sexually. These include the ways children learn about their worth as human beings; about being women and men, and about being individuals; about knowing and protecting the boundaries between themselves and other people; and about dealing with abuse and trauma.

This chapter looks at some of the problems that come up in these four areas.

Self-Esteem: Self-Worth, Self-Confidence, and Self-Respect

Self-esteem has been a popular topic for a while now. It's not just a fad, though. Self-esteem can be thought of as the combination of three important skills: self-worth, self-confidence, and self-respect. How well we learn those three skills has a dramatic effect on many of our problems and solutions. Those skills are at the center of our ability to love and care for ourselves, and to love and care for others.

Self-worth is the belief that we're valuable and worthwhile just as we are. Self-worth doesn't come from anything we do, although many of us grow up believing it will. It doesn't come from achievement. Instead, it comes from loving and accepting ourselves just as we are, with all our strengths and weaknesses. We learn this as children by having others love and accept us just as we are. It also comes from seeing that others love and accept themselves, too.

Self-confidence is the knowledge that we can do what we need to do to survive and to succeed. It's the knowledge that we can take care of ourselves and see that our needs are met. It comes from learning healthy skills, using those skills, and seeing that they can work. It comes from success—and from the willingness to learn from our mistakes. And most of all, it comes from being around people who believe in us.

The Skills of Self-Esteem

- **Self-worth:** I'm valuable and worthwhile just as I am.
- **Self-confidence:** I can do what I need to survive and succeed.
- **Self-respect:** I'm willing to treat myself and others well.

Self-respect is the willingness to treat ourselves well and be treated well. This doesn't mean having everything we want. It means living with dignity and doing what's best for us in the long run. Self-respect comes from knowing that we're worthy of respect, from respecting others, and from the experience of living in harmony with our deepest values.

How Children Learn the Skills of Self-Esteem

The skills of self-esteem can be learned and practiced at any point in life. It's much easier, though, if children learn them from the day they're born. For that to happen, their parents—or other important adults in their lives—have to know and practice those skills. They have to do it consistently, too, so children can learn to believe in it.

Darnell has no trouble with self-esteem. His mother raised him with very little money and even less help, but she knew that the best way to teach a child a skill is to live it. His mother always treated herself and others—even children—with respect. If she made a mistake she admitted it, but she let go of it right away. She let go of other people's mistakes, too—even the ones that hurt. Darnell's mother always seemed to love and accept herself and others just as they were. And it was just as easy for her to let people love her as it was for her to love them.

Children who see this done most of the time learn to believe that they're wonderful and loved. They feel confident and emotionally fulfilled. They treat others well, and they expect the same. When people don't treat them well, they stand up for themselves or get out of the situation quickly.

Of course, many children don't learn these skills. Maybe their parents don't have the skills to pass on to them. Perhaps their parents are weighed down by overwork, money troubles, addiction, violence in the community, or the dozens of other troubles that eat up their energy. Or their parents' efforts to teach these skills might be drowned out by messages that the children hear in their communities, in the popular culture, and among their friends.

Self-Esteem and Sexual Aggression

There's a strong connection between underdeveloped self-esteem and sexual force and manipulation. Some of these examples are common in the old model of relationship:

- the man who makes a game out of getting women into bed, in order to feel more confident
- the woman who thinks she owes a man sex if he spends time and money on her, not really believing she has much to offer a man besides sex
- the man who doesn't take steps to make sure his partner is willing, because he's afraid her saying no would mean he's less of a man
- the woman who is manipulated into having sex, then accuses the man of rape because she's ashamed of having been manipulated
- the man who rapes a woman because he sees her refusal to have sex with him as a put-down
- the woman who struggles but doesn't fight hard or "make a scene" when she's being raped, because she doesn't really believe she's worth protecting
- the woman who doesn't even get angry at being raped, because she doesn't believe that what happens to her matters
- the woman who follows rape with feelings of intense shame, self-blame, and self-hatred

Think of the idea of scarcity—there's not enough to go around—that's so important to the old model. Each of these people believes that he or she is missing something important.

117

Some try to replace that missing part with sex or relationships. Others can't find the strength to protect themselves.

> **People with strong skills in self-esteem don't need to use manipulation. They're also harder to manipulate.**

Of course, many people who have trouble with self-esteem don't fall into these kinds of patterns. They have other problems instead. But people who are skilled in all three areas of self-esteem—self-worth, self-confidence, and self-respect—have no need to use manipulation or force on others. They're also less likely to be taken in by people who do.

Strengthening Self-Esteem Skills

Strengthening self-esteem skills can help us avoid these traps and recover from their effects. There are many forms of therapy that address these problems. The *Worth Protecting* workbook also offers exercises in this. But first, here are some general thoughts.

Please remember that your attitudes toward yourself are things you learned when you were too young to question them and reject the false ones. Now that you have the ability to question and choose, it's your responsibility to do that. Remember that your parents, teachers, family members, and others in your childhood were capable of making big mistakes. They were also raised by people who made mistakes. If you can admit that they were wrong about you, that doesn't mean you're being disloyal. And it doesn't mean you're blaming them. They did the best they could.

Strengthening Self-Esteem Skills

- You took on your attitudes toward yourself when you were too young to question things.
- Now that you have the ability to question and choose, it's your responsibility to do that.
- The people who influenced your self-esteem were capable of being wrong.
- If you admit they were wrong, that doesn't mean you're being disloyal or blaming them.
- While you're learning self-esteem, you can "act as if" you have it.

As mentioned in chapter four, the beliefs about yourself that you learned in childhood are like taped messages that you play over and over in your head. You probably can't shut them off by force of will, but you can tape over them. Every time one of those negative messages comes up, you can correct yourself and say something positive right away.

Amy used to be in the habit of saying "I hate you!" to herself whenever she felt embarrassed or caught herself making a mistake. She'd always done it, as far back as she could remember. She decided to replace this message. Whenever she found herself saying "I hate you," she corrected herself, saying "No, I mean, I **love** you!" That was several years ago. To this day, whenever she feels embarrassed or makes a mistake, a voice goes off inside her head, saying "I love you."

You can also "act as if" you have the skills of self-esteem while you're working on building them. It makes the learning process much more pleasant. Janay was in her mid-thirties when she discovered that the way she thought of herself could affect the way people treated her. As she walked along a city street, she tried pretending that she was someone who had

119

always been cherished by the people closest to her. She pretended she'd been taught nothing but love and respect for herself all her life. She started noticing that, in tiny ways, people were treating her with more respect.

Then Janay tried playing that "game" when she got together with friends and when she saw people in the course of her work. Same thing: people treated her better, so she started feeling better about herself; as a result people started treating her even better. And when anyone got out of line, she could handle it in a calm, balanced way. She still doesn't understand what it all means, but it feels good and she gets more done.

It's as if we're all walking around with "Post-It-Notes" on our foreheads. They tell people how we expect to be treated. Usually we're not even aware that we're sending out any messages, but somehow the messages get across. That's why many people tend to attract the same kinds of partners over and over. It takes effort, but we can change our Post-It-Notes. It takes practice in the skills of self-esteem.

Learning About Gender and Relationship Roles

Our early experiences in our families are often the strongest forces shaping our beliefs about ourselves as men and women, and about our roles in intimate relationships. These kinds of beliefs have a powerful effect on the way we treat others and the way we expect to be treated. The next few pages take a quick look at how girls and boys often take on their beliefs about gender and relationship roles. (Some of these ideas are explained in more detail in Lillian Rubin's book, *Intimate Strangers: Men and Women Together.*)

Becoming Individuals

When babies are born they can't tell the difference between themselves and others. They think each person they see is just another part of them. If they're well cared for, those "parts" seem to bring them what they need as if by magic. But after a few months of life, a baby starts to get the message that other people are actually separate beings, in separate bodies.

That's also when the baby starts to "identify" with someone. Usually it's the main caregiver—the person who spends the most time with the baby. This is most often the baby's mother or another woman, although more and more men are taking that role. This person becomes the baby's main example or image of a human being. Although the baby is starting to understand that the main caregiver is a separate person, he or she thinks of the two of them as being alike—that they're basically one unit. This helps ease the fear of separation.

This identification process is important in helping children develop basic feelings of safety and trust. The child can have serious problems if the main caregiver is abusive, if he or she can't protect the child from abuse or violence, or if he or she can't give the love and care the child needs. These problems with safety and trust often last a lifetime and affect every area of life.

When babies become toddlers they start to "separate" from their main caregivers and think of themselves as individuals. Boys often find it easier to separate from their main caregivers, because so often the caregivers are women. It's easier to separate from someone who's so obviously different.

For the same reason, many girls find it harder to separate. They fear losing that strong connection, as if it might make them lose a part of themselves. Lillian Rubin believes the trouble in separation can make it harder for many women to grow up feeling like individuals. And for some women who have a hard time saying no to men, part of the problem might be the leftover belief that they have to stay connected and please others.

> **Some women have a hard time saying no to men because of an old belief that they have to stay connected and please others.**

The caregivers' own fears and stresses—and their reactions to those fears and stresses—can also affect children's ability to think of themselves as individuals. If the caregivers are afraid of the separation process, they might let go too quickly or too roughly, leaving children feeling unloved or abandoned. Or the caregivers might be so afraid that they try not to let go at all. This also makes it hard for children. They might decide to give up on becoming real individuals because they fear losing the caregiver's love. Or they might have to fight to defend their individuality, then carry that fight on into adult life. That could make it harder for them to give and accept love.

Becoming Women and Men

There are many different ways for children to pick up beliefs about who they are—or who they might be—as women and men. In the family, a child learns by watching the parent and other adults of the same sex. The child also learns from what family members say about his or her being a boy or a girl, and from the way he or she is treated.

In the separation process described above, most boys have an extra task. They've learned to identify with the main caregiver—usually a woman—and now it's time to start seeing themselves as little boys. That means they're different from her in some very important ways. So sometimes they feel as if they have to separate more quickly and more roughly.

Boys often fear their love and identification with a woman, because it feels like a threat to their identity as boys. They might deny their feelings of love and use their anger to separate themselves. Rubin believes this is one reason many boys grow up feeling much more "in touch" with their anger than with their ability to love and care for others. This can happen even if they escape the traditional messages about what it means to be a "real" man.

Children often learn the most about what it means to be a member of their gender by watching the parent of the same sex. If they don't have contact with that parent, they might choose another adult of the same sex, or make up an image of the perfect man or woman. And just as it's impossible to be a perfect parent, it's also impossible to be a perfect gender role model. Many parents who are good people—with the best of intentions—can give their children examples that range from unhealthy to extremely destructive.

Children also learn from the way family members treat them as boys or as girls. If they're treated with consistent love and respect, as important members of the family, children have a better chance of growing up feeling good about their gender. But some children—more often girls—are treated as if they are less valuable, less important, or less intelligent than people of the opposite sex. They might grow up feeling ashamed of who they are. If children are sexually abused, they might grow up believing that people of their sex naturally attract abuse.

Relating to the Opposite Sex

In a family with parents of both genders, a child looks to the parent of the same sex as a role model for relationships with the opposite sex. That parent might treat his or her partner with respect or with disrespect. The parent might be warm and caring or cold and distant—or both at different times. He or she might take a stand when they fight, or give in every time.

123

He or she might act as if the two parents have no sexual or romantic relationship—or act inappropriately sexual in front of the child.

Children study their parents' relationship like a blueprint. Sometimes they take on the same roles as their same-sex parents because they've learned to believe these are the "right" roles for people of their gender. Or they might grow up swearing, "I'll never act like that!" For example, if the parent of their gender abuses his or her power over the other parent, they might decide never to do that. Then as teens or adults they might find themselves doing some of the same things with their partners, only in different ways. Or they might swing too far in the other direction and let their partners have too much power over them.

> **Children watch how their parents relate. They might decide that's the right way—or decide it's all wrong, but still find themselves acting the same way.**

The experience children have with parents or other family members of the opposite sex is also very important. Both girls and boys need relationships that are loving, respectful, and safe—not sexual, and not physically or emotionally abusive. Children whose relationships with their opposite-sex parents are troubled often grow up to have troubled relationships with people of the opposite sex.

Children also take on definite roles in their families, and carry those roles into teen and adult life. There the roles can affect their ability to communicate well with partners or to stay safe in dating situations. One example would be the training that many little boys get in holding back their feelings. Later in life that training can make it much harder to talk about what they do and don't want from their partners. Another example would be the training that many little girls get in being cute and "flirting" with adults. In a safe family that kind of role might win nothing but attention and affection for a child. But in teen or adult life it can also get people into trouble.

The Need to Resolve

There's also something called the "need to resolve." It often affects the kinds of people and relationships we tend to attract, or be attracted to. In many people's childhood there was a particular experience, or a particular relationship, that was especially troubling or traumatic. It might have been a parent, a sister or brother, etc. Sometimes in adult life we'll find ourselves attracting people who are like that person in some important ways, or relationships or experiences that are like the one that caused us many problems so long ago.

Without being aware of it, we sometimes try to make our childhood experiences happen again in another form, to see if we can make them come out differently.

We're not aware of it, but somewhere inside us we know that we haven't resolved—finished with or made peace with—our experiences. Something in us is trying to make those experiences happen again in another form, so we can make them come out differently. Unfortunately, reliving painful experiences doesn't resolve them. It often adds new wounds to the old ones. But that doesn't stop us from getting into the same kinds of situations over and over.

Real resolution comes from getting help, taking an honest and compassionate look at our past, and learning to do things differently. Trying on new, healthy relationship patterns is uncomfortable at first. But that discomfort leads to insights that we'd never have if we stayed stuck in the same drama.

Boundaries

If we're born not seeing the difference between ourselves and other people, then a big lifelong task is mapping out the boundaries that divide our lives from the lives of other people. This includes the boundaries between our thoughts, emotions, bodies, responsibilities, identities, freedom, and territory. Healthy boundaries are important to sexual safety.

Children learn to draw and respect these boundary lines by watching their parents draw and respect them. Healthy boundaries are both strong and flexible. They make it possible for people to see where they should set limits for their own behavior and the way others treat them. Clear boundaries are also guidelines we can use in deciding whether problems are ours or somebody else's.

The Two Extremes

There are two main dangers as children go through the process of learning to draw boundaries.

One danger is that children won't learn to draw these lines, or they'll learn to draw weak lines that cave in easily. Maybe their parents drew weak boundaries, and the children followed their example. Or maybe parents invaded the children's boundaries so often that the children grew up with no sense of having their own "territory." They grew up believing they had no way of keeping anyone out—or that they had no right to do so. This often happens in cases of abuse. Children can grow into adults who have little or no defense against abuse and control by others.

The other danger is that children will draw lines so hard and rigid that they seal themselves off from others. They feel alienated from others—cut off, guarded, and different. They don't feel free to show their more vulnerable feelings, and they're afraid of others' feelings. They feel a desperate need to control and defend their little world, so they learn to control and manipulate other people. People with rigid boundaries may have strong spiritual or religious beliefs, but they often have a hard time feeling a true sense of spiritual connection with others. That would make them feel too vulnerable.

Boundaries in Women's Lives

Women are more likely to be abused as adults than men are. One reason for that is that many women have a harder time drawing clear, definite boundaries between their lives and the lives of others. Many little girls learn to communicate in ways that are more subtle, less direct, and less obvious than little boys' communication styles. Girls are often more aware of social obligations and complications than boys are. Many girls learn to be diplomatic and to try not to upset others.

Mary has always had a hard time saying no. When a man gets too close to her sexual boundaries, she'll do anything she can think of to distract him. She'll ask for another glass of wine, or bring up a subject that she knows he'd like to talk about. But she never thinks of just saying, "Please stop doing that. I don't want you to do that." She's afraid of hurting his feelings or that he'll think she's too bossy or socially clumsy. All her life she's learned to say things in indirect ways, believing that's the best way to be careful and considerate. But the guys aren't hearing her say no because she's not saying it in a language that they can understand.

Some women don't protect their boundaries because of messages they've heard all their lives from family members, friends, television, and other influences. Those messages have made it harder for them to see themselves as separate individuals who have a right to protect their "space." Women are also more likely to have been sexually abused as children. Sexual abuse is a serious invasion of a child's boundaries. It can make it harder for people to recognize and protect themselves when others invade their boundaries later in life.

Whatever the causes, a lack of clear boundary skills can make a woman more vulnerable to rape and manipulation. Rape is a direct, forceful invasion of personal boundaries. Manipulation is more subtle, but it's also a boundary invasion. If a woman has a problem with boundaries, she might be more vulnerable to being manipulated, or she might learn to use manipulation on others.

When women learn to define and communicate clear limits, they become less vulnerable to sexual force and manipulation. They even appear less vulnerable on the outside. No matter how attractive these women might be, the men who are looking for sexually vulnerable women will be more likely to pass them by.

When women learn good boundary skills, they also become more aware when someone is trying to invade their boundaries. People who rape and manipulate sometimes start out by invading boundaries a little at a time—long before they make their final moves. They start out with small violations, to test the reaction. Then they back off, but they invade a little farther the next time. If a woman is more aware of her boundaries, she's more likely to notice those little invasions before the situation gets violent. The sooner she sees the warning signs, the better her chance of getting out safely.

Boundaries in Men's Lives

Women aren't the only ones who sometimes have trouble finding and protecting their boundaries. Men can also have histories that leave them confused about where their rights and responsibilities begin and end. And far more men were sexually abused in childhood than we ever imagined.[1] Many men have the added complication of having been taught all their lives that they're supposed to be all-powerful. When their boundaries are invaded, it feels like a denial of their basic worth as men.

Common Boundary Issues for Men

- Many men are taught to defend their boundaries with aggression.
- Men with poor boundary skills might not even notice others' boundaries.
- Men with rigid boundaries have a hard time caring what others feel.

It's true that more men than women have been trained to react with anger when someone crosses their boundaries. That can make boundaries operate like minefields, especially for men who've never learned about the concept of boundaries. They might find themselves "blowing up" just because someone asks an innocent question, but not knowing why they're doing it. They might not have learned any other skills for defending their privacy.

And in men as in women, a lack of clear boundary skills can make people less likely to notice and respect other people's boundaries. Men who have problems with their own boundaries might fall into patterns of sexual force and manipulation. They might not think of their actions in those terms. They might not even be aware that there are boundaries to be crossed.

If a man's childhood led him to develop rigid boundaries, he might never develop "empathy" skills. Those are the skills that let people know and care about what others are feeling. He might manipulate, rape, or otherwise abuse women because he's afraid to see them as human beings whose feelings matter. The idea of empathizing with others' emotions—or even feeling anything besides anger—is terrifying to him.

If you're a man who has a history of abusing others, you might have strong legal, moral, or emotional reasons for wanting to learn better ways of relating. If you're willing to get help, and if you have the courage to develop your empathy skills, you have a good chance of becoming the man you were born to be. The book *Men's Work*, by Paul Kivel, is an excellent place to start. So are men's therapy groups and counselors in your community.

Like self-esteem skills, boundary skills can be learned and practiced at any point in life. It might start out as a difficult process, but it gets much easier. When boundaries are both strong and flexible, people find that they have more fun, freedom, and safety than they could ever have imagined. Life is much better without all that pain and fear.

The Effects of Trauma and Abuse

In a sad way, it makes sense that people who were hurt or abused in childhood would be more likely to be abused—or learn to abuse others—as teens and adults. Although most people who survive childhood trauma and abuse don't grow up to take on the roles of victims or abusers, some do. In these cases, it's important to look at the possible connection between childhood experiences and adult patterns. But it's also important to remember that childhood experiences don't force us to follow the same patterns when we grow up. We always have choices, and many people make healthy choices against incredible odds.

One common effect of child abuse and violence in the home, or violence in the community, is emotional trauma. Trauma might be described as an intense fear or shock. Emotional trauma is a reaction to pain that makes it hard for us to recover from the experience. Trauma doesn't happen just because of painful events or circumstances in children's lives. It happens because children don't have the kind of help they need to work through the emotions connected with those events.

> **Emotional trauma happens when children don't have the kind of help they need to work through the emotions connected with painful events in their lives.**

Many events and conditions might cause trauma if the child doesn't have the right kind of help in coping with them. These conditions can include physical, sexual, or emotional abuse by parents or other family members; or the effects of alcoholism or other addiction in the family. They can also include violence in the community, the death of a parent or other loved one, a parent's mental illness, the permanent injury or long illness of a parent, or seeing a parent convicted of crime and sent to prison. Children who have surgery or long hospitalization can also suffer trauma.

Trauma can result if children don't get the help they need when their parents are divorced, and during the years before divorce when they watch their parents struggle in conflict. Children also can suffer trauma from the effects of poverty or a parent's unemployment, or from the effects of prejudice and discrimination in the community and society as a whole.

What Makes It Trauma?

Of course, children can and do heal from these and other painful experiences. But this is much more likely to happen if there's someone there who can help them talk about how they feel, understand that their feelings are valid and normal, and comfort and resolve the feelings.[2]

If the family and the community react to the painful experience by denying it or keeping the child from talking about it, the child will suffer trauma. The child will have no way to confirm and understand his or her feelings. Most often those feelings will be flatly denied. The child will feel crazy. This is very common in addicted families and in cases of sexual abuse.

Some people who suffer trauma develop a psychological illness called "post-traumatic stress disorder" (PTSD). This illness can have many long-lasting symptoms, including intense fear, difficulty sleeping, anger or rage, guilt, numbness, depression, nightmares and flashbacks (strong memories of the event), problems with concentration or memory, and substance abuse or other addictive behaviors. PTSD comes from the experience of trauma along with a combination of emotional and brain-chemical reactions.

> **Some children react to abuse by taking on victim roles, learning to victimize others, or relating sexually when it's not safe or appropriate.**

Trauma forms a deep wound, a hole that people often try to fill with whatever seems logical to them at the time. This might be alcohol or other drugs, sex, overeating, work, money, control, religion, success—you name it. But these things don't fill in the hole. Some of them—like alcohol, drugs, sexual carelessness, and overeating—only dig it deeper.

Childhood Abuse and Sexual Aggression

There can be a strong connection between abuse in childhood—particularly sexual abuse—and sexual force or manipulation later in life. Abuse in childhood can teach a child to see the world as a place where people are victimized. The physical and/or sexual abuse is painful and scary, but it becomes familiar. Some adults never learn to see danger coming or protect themselves. They've taken on the identities of victims, and they don't see any other choice.

A child who's been physically abused can also learn that violence is the way to relate to other people, either as a victim or as someone who uses violence against others. Trying to understand it all, the child might decide that using violence is his or her only chance of staying safe.

Some children who have been sexually abused learn to relate sexually even when it's more appropriate to relate in other ways. As adults they might still have a tendency to flirt or act in sexual ways, even in situations where those actions aren't safe. They might not be aware that's what they're doing. This sends the wrong message. Most partners will just react with confusion, jealousy, or bruised egos. But some might react with manipulation or violence. Laid on top of the unhealed wounds from childhood, the effects of this new aggression might be devastating.

"It Was My Fault."

Children are designed to try to make sense of what's happening to them. Abuse of a child is hard for the smartest adult to understand. The task is many times more difficult for a child. Without honest, caring adults there to help them work through their feelings, children develop their own explanations for what happened. Those explanations might appear to make sense at first. They might even help children feel safer, but they can cause great pain as children's lives progress.

Why Do Children Blame Themselves?
They think:
- If the abuse is their fault, it must be under their control.
- If it's under their control, then they're not powerless against it.
- If they're not powerless, life won't be so scary.

For a child who's being abused, or living in the pain of a traumatic situation, it's terrifying to admit that the situation is beyond his or her control. Children often react by blaming themselves, deciding that they're "bad." They think that, if the painful situation is their fault, then it must be under their control. If it's under their control, then they're not powerless. Then the fear isn't so horrible. But the self-blame locks them into humiliation, the first stage of the old, destructive model of relationship.

As time passes, they continue to blame themselves. Some children come to believe that they deserve abuse and so don't learn the skills of self-protection. There may be no healthy, caring adult around to teach these skills. Children are often unaware of these beliefs. They don't understand how their beliefs affect their thoughts, feelings, and actions. Children and adults need help in looking at their beliefs about themselves and replacing the ones that don't work with more realistic ones.

Another complication comes from the fact that the person who is abusing the child is often someone the child loves very much. Children have a basic need to love and be loyal to the people who take care of them. In many cases children learn to be loyal to people they can't trust—people they know will abuse them. The child might learn that love and abuse go together—that the hand that brings the pain is also the hand that takes it away. If this pattern continues into adulthood, it can give an abusive partner tremendous power.

Denial

Denial is a common survival skill for children in troubled families. Denial might be thought of as an ability to know something and, at the same time, not know it. It's an ability to believe that serious problems don't exist—or that they aren't as bad as they really are.

Sometimes the pain children face is too great for them to cope with. And sometimes they'd be in danger if they were to confront other family members with the truth about their lives. Denial can keep children safe while they're still young and vulnerable.

This may be an important survival skill for children, but it can cause problems as children grow into adults. There are many ways that denial can raise the risk of sexual force and manipulation. For example, denial often keeps people from getting help for problems with alcohol and other drugs. People who abuse these substances are often more likely to use sexual force or manipulation, or less able to protect themselves.

Denial can also put people out of touch with their feelings. Many women who have been raped by acquaintances report that, before the rape, they had "gut" feelings that told them something was wrong. They ignored those feelings or convinced themselves that the feelings were wrong.[4] For some, denial learned in childhood might well have played a part in that process.

Denial can keep children safe while they're young but cause big problems as they grow into teens or adults—particularly if they drink or use drugs.

Resiliency—Strength and Flexibility

With all the pain and trauma that so many children live through, how do most of them grow up to lead healthy lives? Some people who have studied children talk about "resiliency factors"—people, places, and opportunities that help children grow strong and flexible. Resiliency factors don't make the pain and fear of abuse and trauma go away. But they do help children heal their wounds and learn to live.

Many people with troubled childhood histories never get involved in destructive or self-destructive activities. They never abuse alcohol or other drugs, they have satisfying careers, and they have nothing but safe and respectful relationships. Many others get involved in self-destructive activities for a little while. Then they get tired of the pain and do whatever they need to do to get their lives in order.

> **The pain that children live through doesn't sentence them to live as victims or victimizers. Human beings have many amazing ways of healing.**

What are some of the childhood resiliency factors that sowed the seeds of that basic strength? In many children's lives there's at least one sane, respectful adult who really cares. It doesn't have to be a parent. It can be a grandparent, teacher, neighbor, or anyone. These adults accept children exactly as they are and show them their strengths. Sometimes these adults also help children find the strength in their cultures of origin and in the many cultural traditions that can help them cope with life.

Some children become resilient by having a safe place to go where they can feel removed from the pain at home or in the community. Some children learn to express their feelings through make-believe and through art, music, drama, or writing. They can grieve their losses and find healing through creativity. Many children learn to escape life's pain in healthy interests and projects, in school, or in their communities. They can find a sense of purpose, connection with the community, and the knowledge that their minds can work well even if their emotions are painful.[5] Resilient children don't always escape trouble in adult life. Many go through more than a few bumps and scrapes before they settle into peaceful, productive lives. But it's important to remember that resiliency exists. The pain that children live through doesn't sentence them to live as victims or victimizers. Human beings have many amazing ways of healing.

Getting Help for Childhood Wounds

Whether or not they increase the risk of sexual force and manipulation, the effects of childhood abuse are serious. They're far too complicated to address in depth as a small part of this book. If you were or may have been abused in childhood, it's important to get professional help. There are therapists in your community who specialize in the effects of childhood abuse.

If one of the wounds of childhood is a substance-abuse problem, it's important to get help for that problem first. Abuse of alcohol and other drugs is dangerous. It raises the risk of being hurt sexually or hurting others. It also gets in the way of any therapy and group work you might be doing to resolve childhood issues.

There are many happy, emotionally healthy adults who have worked hard to overcome the effects of childhood trauma and abuse. Their job wasn't easy—and sometimes it still isn't—but they've learned to stop hurting themselves and others. They're building successful lives and happy, loving relationships. All these things once seemed impossible to them. If you're a survivor of childhood abuse or trauma, please remember that this hope is yours, too.

Journal Questions

1. Have you ever deliberately tried to improve your confidence or knowledge of your own self-worth? How did you do that? What were the results?

2. When you were a young child, how easy or difficult was it for you to see yourself as an individual? How easy or difficult was it for you to identify with others of your gender?

3. In your home when you were growing up, what kinds of boundaries did your family members draw? What boundaries did you learn to draw?

4. Was there anyone in your childhood who helped you talk about your feelings, accept your feelings, and understand that those feelings made sense?

5. What did your childhood teach you to believe about yourself as a man or woman, and about your true worth as a human being?

Notes

1. Several of the books in the Bibliography address childhood sexual abuse. Two that focus on sexual abuse of boys are Stephen Grubman-Black's *Broken Boys/Mending Men* and Mic Hunter's *Abused Boys.*
2. This concept came from Cathleen Brooks's description in Breaking the Chain, published by the Illinois Prevention Resource Center (a project of Prevention First, Inc.). The Bibliography lists many excellent books on childhood abuse, trauma, and resiliency.
3. Many of the books listed in the Bibliography address post-traumatic stress reactions. Two that focus on PTSD are Raymond Flannery's *Post-Traumatic Stress Disorder* and Frank Parkinson's *Post-Trauma Stress.*
4. The literature on date and acquaintance rape frequently mentions this denial of important "gut" feelings. For examples, you might start with I Never Called It Rape or *Acquaintance Rape: The Hidden Crime.*
5. The literature on resiliency is exciting and has a lot of good information that adults can use in their own healing processes. You might start with Linda Sanford's Strong at the Broken Places. Many books on childhood abuse also address resiliency.

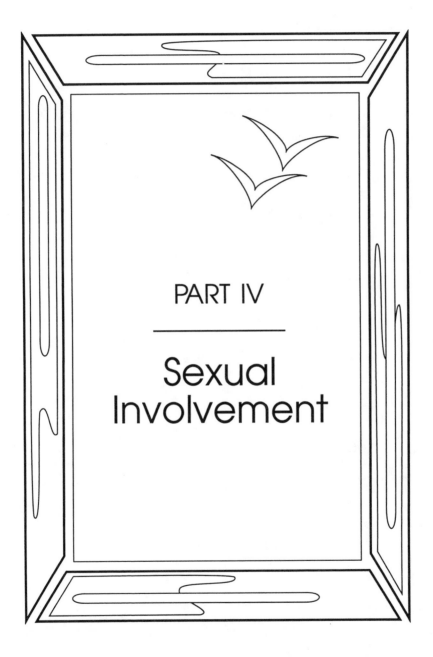

PART IV

Sexual
Involvement

CHAPTER 8

Communication in Sexual Involvement

Now that we know who the actors are, it's time to look at the script. Parts II and III have shown experiences that can raise people's risk of sexual force and manipulation. These experiences include confusion and conflict about what the rules are and what people want from one another. They also include messages from primitive brain centers and from earlier civilizations.

More confusion comes into play when people get messages from the popular culture that set both women and men up as commodities to be gotten and used. On top of that there are unresolved issues from childhood, including a lack of skills in self-esteem, sex-role conflicts, weak or rigid boundaries, and other effects of trauma and abuse.

Communication in the Old and New Models

This chapter looks at communication in sexual situations—or in situations that one or more people would like to think of as sexual. There are two kinds of communication: healthy and unhealthy.

Healthy communication comes from the kinds of beliefs and thought patterns described in the new model of relationship. It leads to the friendship and respect that bring the new model full circle. Unhealthy communication comes from the fear-based beliefs and thought patterns described in the old model. It leads to panic, power games, and victimization.

In the new model, sexual communication is

- based on self-knowledge
- clear and direct
- respectful
- assertive
- appropriate for the situation
- not drunk or high
- sometimes a little clumsy

This chapter looks at these qualities.

Sexual Limits

In healthy sexual communication, one of our most important aims is to set clear limits on what is and isn't going to happen. Limits aren't the same as boundaries, but they're related. As described in chapter seven, a boundary is where each one of us begins and ends—our feelings, our responsibilities, our bodies, etc.

A limit is the line we draw that lets people know what they have to do to respect our boundaries. For example, you can set limits that protect your emotional boundaries. You might do that by asking someone not to say sarcastic things to you. Or you might protect one of your physical boundaries by asking someone not to put his or her arm around you.

Verbal and Nonverbal Communication

Communication isn't done just with words. There are many nonverbal forms of communication, including facial expressions, body language, tones of voice, etc. Although we tend to think we rely on verbal communication (words), nonverbal communication often has the strongest effect. That's because we aren't always aware that we're picking it up. We don't question what it's saying to us—or our reactions to it. It's more subtle, so we have less defense against it.

Most of us have been taught that it's better not to "spoil the mood" by talking about sexual desires and limits in direct words. And there may be times when nonverbal signals are enough to get the point across. But it's not worth the risk of rape, manipulation, AIDS, unwanted pregnancy, and the whole list of other problems that can follow mistakes in this area.

> **It's important to use words in sexual communication. Nothing you could say would "spoil the mood" as badly as rape, unwanted pregnancy, or life-threatening disease.**

It's absolutely necessary to be able to speak honestly and openly about sexual expectations. Knowing how and when to use direct words is an important survival skill. Nothing you could say would ever spoil the mood as badly as rape, unwanted pregnancy, or life-threatening disease.

Here are some guidelines for healthy sexual communication in the new model of relationship.

New-Model Communication

Communication Based on Self-Knowledge

Before we can communicate in healthy ways, we have to know what we want and don't want, what we feel and don't feel, what we expect, and where our limits are. We have to know what we're willing to do to clarify and protect those limits, and how to react with dignity if our wishes are disappointed. It's hard to be honest if we don't know what the truth is. It's hard to keep our balance when we've been taken completely by surprise. That's why knowledge of our own wants, needs, and limits is such an important part of the new model.

When people are getting to know one another in a dating situation, it's important for both partners to know what their sexual limits are. A woman in particular needs to ask herself—before she even gets together with a man—how far she's willing to let the relationship go that day. If she's not sure what she wants, she'll have a hard time communicating it to him. She may give him mixed signals, which might cause anything from frustration to danger.

The man she's dating also needs to ask himself what level of sexual involvement he wants. He has just as much right as she does to take things slowly and carefully. He needs to be ready to communicate his wishes clearly and give his partner a chance to react according to her own wishes.

If one partner is going to ask for sexual involvement, he or she needs to be prepared for the possibility that the other might not want the same level of involvement. If the other partner says no, how can the first partner accept the refusal without feeling like he or she has been judged to be inferior? The skills of self-esteem are important ones to learn and practice before we even get together with a prospective partner.

> **Before we can communicate clearly, we need to know what we want, need, feel, and expect. We need to know our own limits.**

When we're disappointed, sometimes it's better to express our disappointment in words, and sometimes it's better to keep it to ourselves. A lot depends on our level of trust, our basic personality style, and the situation. Before we ask, it helps to think about how we want to react if we're turned down. Which choice would leave us feeling more dignified and better about ourselves?

In general, most of us have a lot of expectations of other people, especially people who are attractive to us. These aren't limited to sexual expectations. They have to do with the way people dress, talk, think, act, drive, eat—you name it. We usually don't even realize that these are our expectations. We just think it's the way people are supposed to be.

The more we can identify our own expectations, the easier it becomes to tell the difference between our legitimate limits and our desire to control other people. The more we realize that other people have a duty to respect our limits—but not to live up to our image of "perfect people"—the better our relationships will be.[1]

Clear and Direct Communication

Sexual involvement is an area of life where confusion can cause problems that ruin relationships, destroy lives, or kill people. The best way to avoid confusion is to communicate directly—to say exactly what we mean. This means never assuming others know what we want and don't want, or that we know what they want. In other words, it means taking

147

responsibility for saying what we want and don't want, and for asking what our partners want.

In clear and direct communication, people are honest. We use words that leave no doubt about their meaning. For example, "I want to spend some intimate time with you" could mean a number of things. One person might hear it as, "I want to cuddle up by the fire and talk about how we feel about each other," while another might mean it as, "I want to have sex with you." If they don't get more specific, they're headed for trouble.

In direct communication we paint a word-picture of what we want and don't want. But it's like a clear photograph, not a blurry painting where different people see different things. If the blurry painting sounds more romantic, it's probably because all our lives people have been telling us that confusion was romantic. Chances are some of those people thought they had something to gain from keeping things confused. The trouble is there's even more to lose.[2]

We need to take responsibility for saying what we want and don't want, and for asking what our partners want.

As mentioned in the last chapter, many women have grown up learning to communicate their limits in more subtle, indirect ways. They might have been told that direct communication is too harsh or too masculine. Or maybe they've even been discouraged in more subtle ways, like a show of disapproval from parents or friends. So they might feel uncomfortable coming right out and saying what they want or don't want. Using direct words to set limits might make them feel as if they're being rude. But often they're communicating with

148

men who have been trained in a more direct style of communication. Direct words may be the only effective way of getting the message across.[3]

This doesn't mean that the way women were trained to communicate is wrong and the way men were trained is right. It's just as important for men to learn to understand women's indirect messages as it is for women to learn to give direct ones. But indirect communication often leads to misunderstanding, and rape and manipulation are more likely to take place in an atmosphere of misunderstanding. A woman has a better chance of staying safe if she learns the skills of direct communication. And her safety is much more important than who's right or wrong.

Respect for Ourselves and Others

One of the things we often forget when we're trying to communicate desires and limits is the need to show respect—for ourselves and for others. Even with the best intentions we can fail to show respect. All we have to do is rush things, speak out of defensiveness, insult people, or fail to respect people's cultural norms.

A couple has been dating for two months, and it's the end of dinner on the sixth date. At that point it might seem quite respectful for one partner to say, "I'd really like to make love with you tonight." But what if he or she made that statement five minutes after they met? As the next chapter will show, there's a natural timing and building process in sexual communication. If we try to cut corners, we risk being disrespectful.

We also tend to be less respectful when we feel defensive. Sometimes we're afraid of setting limits. Maybe we weren't raised to see limit-setting as something we deserve to do. Maybe our boundaries weren't respected when we were children, so we assume they won't be respected now. Whatever the cause, when we try to set limits it comes out sounding like an accusation.

Sarah wondered why Brad was offended on their first date when she gave him a reasonable set of ground rules for their relationship. After all, she didn't know him very well. She was just trying to protect herself. But the trouble was that she communicated those ground rules in a stern and accusing way.

Brad called a few weeks later and explained how he felt about that evening. He said that at the time she might have been thinking, "I don't know you," but her words, timing, tone of voice, and body language all told him, "You can't be trusted." After they ended their phone conversation Sarah started wondering how she would feel if someone—her boss, for example—explained the ground rules for a project that way. She had to admit that she'd feel angry and humiliated.

Even with good intentions we can fail to show respect. All we have to do is rush things, be defensive, insult people, or fail to respect their cultures.

Setting limits doesn't have to be done in a defensive way. It doesn't have to sound like an accusation. The more respect we show, the more we attract respect. Acting suspicious and unfriendly might push people away, but it won't make them respect us. And if the person we're feeling suspicious of has a tendency to be hostile, our suspicion might make him or her feel more hostile.

If you believe someone is likely to hurt you or take advantage of you, then it's important to get away from that person as soon as possible. But if you don't have any reason to believe that—not even a gut feeling about it—then treat that person like a friend. You can still make sure you stay safe. You can still be honest about what you want and don't want. But you can do these things without being disrespectful.

Men may have been trained to try to be powerful, but many feel powerless when it comes to dating. They're scared of asking for dates or sexual involvement, because a woman's refusal feels like a rejection—not just a rejection of the activity, but a rejection of their worth and their manhood. They feel very vulnerable. The more respect a woman shows in refusing, the more likely the man is to feel that his self-respect hasn't been damaged, and the less likely he is to react with anger or force. Even if a man wants sex, that probably isn't all he wants. He wants to be liked and respected, too.

It's easy to insult people without meaning to—and sometimes without even noticing it. In many families, cultures, and social groups people get in the habit of playfully picking on one another. There's no harm meant, and often it's a way of showing acceptance and affection. But for someone who's not used to it, this verbal "sparring" can appear insulting. And even if people are used to them, some kinds of humor—like sarcasm, for example—will damage people's feelings of trust and worth in the relationship.

And then there are the "isms"—like racism, classism, or sexism aimed at either gender. The problem isn't that these things aren't "politically correct." The problem is that they're insulting. And they're not necessary. In the new model people don't say or do things out of prejudice. Plenty of help is available for working through those prejudices and the experiences that led to them. We don't have to take our prejudices out on others.

It's important to respect the other person's family culture and culture of origin. In some families and cultures, people are open and matter-of-fact in talking about sex. In others, people are more reserved, and it's considered disrespectful to be too direct or too specific about it. In some cultures, any direct communication is considered impolite.

If you're dating someone whose family or cultural background is different from yours, please don't assume your partner feels the same as you about sexual communication. Find out what the norms and customs are. Find out what that culture considers respectful and disrespectful. Talk to your partner about how he or she feels about sexual communication. Find a common language.

Of course, that doesn't mean we shouldn't set clear verbal limits if our partners are from families or cultures that don't like to talk about sex. It just means we do a little extra work in showing that we respect people, their families, and their cultures.

And finally, the respect we show ourselves will also have a strong effect on our partners' respect for us. This doesn't mean being stuck up or arrogant. It means accepting our dignity. It means never forgetting that we're worthy. It can make a big difference.

Assertive Messages

Some forms of direct communication are also called "assertive." Assertive messages are direct, definite statements that we make even though others might not want to hear them. They're often clear, simple statements of what we want or don't want, believe or don't believe, and will or won't allow. They're made with respect for ourselves and others.

An assertive statement isn't a statement of anger or defense, although we can make assertive statements even when we're angry. But we don't have to be angry—or act angry—to be assertive. The most effective assertive statements are ones that are made in a calm, matter-of-fact tone of voice. There's no bad will, just a desire to set clear limits.

Being assertive isn't the same as being aggressive, passive, or using "passive aggression." Here's a breakdown of all these terms:

Unlike people who are being assertive, people who are being **aggressive** aren't just trying to communicate. Aggression is meant to force people into things, hurt them, take advantage of them, make them mad, or get back at them. If you're yelling, hitting someone, or calling the person names, you're probably being aggressive instead of assertive. You may succeed in forcing or getting back at the person, but the force will get in your way. It often keeps someone from understanding or accepting the point you want to get across.

When people are being **passive**, they choose to do nothing and hope that others will get the message. Unfortunately, if the other people are being aggressive, they'll usually get whatever message they want to get—no matter what message the passive person means to send. If you have important wants, needs, or limits that you're not stating—even though the time is right to state them—then you're being passive. People can't hear what you're *not* saying, so your needs or limits probably won't be respected. And *you* probably won't be respected as much as you would if you made a direct statement.

> **Assertiveness is a wonderful tool. It sets us free. It cuts through passivity, and gives a dignified way of answering aggression and passive aggression.**

When people are being **passive-aggressive**, they're trying to force, hurt, or insult people in sneaky ways—without taking responsibility for it. Passive aggression is a kind of manipulation. It often hurts the person who's doing it more than the other person. If you're being sarcastic, sulking, refusing to talk to someone, trying to make them feel guilty, or not doing what you promised to do, then you're probably being passive-aggressive. There's something important that you need to say, but you're afraid to say it. The passive aggression won't change things for the better. You'll stay angry and frustrated until you learn to communicate more directly. Assertiveness is a wonderful tool. It sets us free. It cuts through passivity, and gives a dignified way of answering aggression and passive aggression. In assertiveness, we take responsibility for our own thoughts, feelings, actions, needs, and limits. And we don't accept responsibility for anyone else's.

People who are aggressive or manipulative are playing games. Assertiveness is the best way of *not* playing the game—and that's the only way to win.

Staying Appropriate for the Situation

In the new model of relationship, we get to know one another slowly and carefully. We understand that not everyone is a good candidate for close friend or lover. We're willing to wait to see if it's safe before we start telling the other person too much about ourselves.

It helps to think of each person as having three "selves" or "zones," like circles around one another. The outside circle is the "public self," the one that anybody can get to know. The middle circle is the "private self," the one that's there for good friends who have earned our trust. The inner circle is the "intimate self." Very few people in our whole lives get into that circle, because there we're most vulnerable.

In the new model of relationship, we start out by staying in the public self. We talk about safe topics—our work, our favorite activities, music, movies, books, etc. For example, a woman is careful not to give out her phone number or address too soon. She knows that if a man is interested—and emotionally healthy—he'll be willing to give her *his* phone number until she feels safe with him.

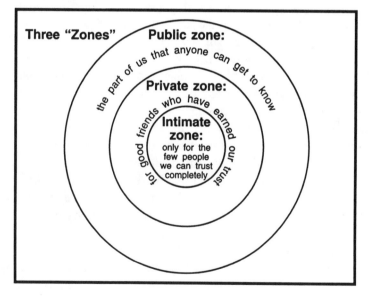

Three "Zones"

Public zone: the part of us that anyone can get to know

Private zone: for good friends who have earned our trust

Intimate zone: only for the few people we can trust completely

When we're still in our public selves, we don't start talking about highly personal subjects—like problems in past relationships or difficult childhood experiences. Even though we want to know one another better, we value each person's privacy and respect each person's boundaries.

When we're caught up in the old model, though, we might tend to communicate far too much, far too soon. We often start talking about past relationships and childhood trauma on the first date. This creates a false sense of closeness between us.

Some people use this false sense of closeness to manipulate others or make them feel safer than they really are. It creates a feeling of obligation: "I've told you everything about me. Now what about you?" Pretty soon it's, "I feel like I know you so well, and we've gotten so close. All that's keeping us apart are these clothes. . . ."

Many women who have been raped on dates report that the men who raped them first created a false feeling of intimacy. These men told very personal stories about their lives and invited the women to do the same. If someone you're dating pushes the communication into the private zone too quickly, watch out. Don't tell him or her anything personal about yourself. Steer the conversation back to the public zone. And stay in public places until you know the person well and you're sure that he or she can be trusted.

When Marilyn was on her first (and only) date with Ron, she made sure they took separate cars and met in a busy restaurant. Over dinner he started talking about his father in a way that made it clear to her that he really hated his father. She could tell that his hatred for his father was a serious problem for him. She could also tell that he didn't have a very good sense of boundaries or appropriateness.

Marilyn got a gut feeling that Ron wasn't a healthy person, and she started to feel very uncomfortable with him. She excused herself, went to the ladies' room, and stayed there a long time. When she came back to the table, she told him she was feeling very sick. She apologized, excused herself, and left the restaurant alone. She never went out with him again.

Pushing into the private zone isn't always a sign of physical danger, but it's usually a reason to use caution. Sometimes people will tell too much, too soon, because they don't know any better. Many people—particularly people who were raised in troubled families—think that if they don't "tell all" they're not being honest. People who are new in therapy or recovery from addiction might feel that they have to explain their lives or behavior by telling about their past experiences.

Many women who have been raped on dates say the men first created a false feeling of intimacy. They told personal stories and asked personal questions.

These are important signs. People who have a hard time handling communication often have a hard time handling relationships in general. They might not be rapists or manipulators, but they might still make difficult partners. And people who are new in therapy or recovery from addiction are often very vulnerable. They may not be ready for healthy sexual involvement. And if they're newly clean and sober, sexual or romantic experiences might lead to relapse.

To stay in the new model and keep communication healthy, it helps to remember the public, private, and intimate zones. You can move slowly and carefully from one zone to the next, and only when time and mutual experiences have told you it's safe to do so.

Staying Clean and Sober

It's hard to move slowly and carefully through the stages of involvement when one or both partners are drinking or using other drugs. Healthy communication means that people are capable of sending and receiving clear messages, and setting and respecting boundaries. People who want to be safe and respectful together avoid getting drunk or high.

Under the influence of alcohol or other drugs, people tend to pass through the stages of involvement more quickly. Women often agree to more activity than they'd choose if they were able to watch out for themselves. Alcohol and other drugs make it harder for people to communicate clearly and notice the messages others are sending. They also make it easier for people to mistake the messages they do pick up. The effects of these drugs make it easier for some people to get aggressive—even violent. And under the influence many women find it harder to see danger coming or to know and protect their own sexual boundaries and limits.

Men who plan to manipulate or force women into sex often use alcohol and other drugs as part of their scheme. Usually this is designed to bring the woman's defenses down. Many women report having been raped when they were drinking, or after they'd passed out.

In some cases a man will keep buying drinks or drugs to make a woman feel obligated to him. Particularly if the drugs are expensive, the man usually sees them as having a sexual "price." If a man tries to talk a woman into accepting drinks or drugs, that's a clear sign of danger. If she wants to protect herself, she needs to refuse what he's offering and take steps to avoid being alone with him. Rape is too high a price for any high—and it's certainly too high a price for being polite.

Both men and women sometimes believe they're not responsible for the things they do when they're drunk or high.

That belief is false. Maybe they can't always control or predict their actions when they're under the influence, but they do have the choice not to drink or use drugs when there's a risk of sexual manipulation or force.

Alcohol and other drugs

- block out important messages
- make it easier to mistake messages
- make some people more aggressive
- make it harder for others to protect themselves
- are sometimes thought of as having a sexual "price"
- make it easier to deny responsibility for our actions

If you've tried to make a choice not to drink or use drugs but you've ended up drinking or using anyway, you probably need help. Chapter thirteen goes into more detail on this subject.

Awkwardness in Healthy Communication

With all that said, please remember this: Not all people who don't communicate well are manipulators or aggressors. Some are just a little clumsy when they're talking to people who are attractive to them. They might be nervous, out of practice, or low on self-confidence. Many perfectly attractive people feel perfectly unattractive. They might even work hard to look like they're not interested and miss the most obvious signs of interest from others.

When a relationship is just getting started, people's insecurities might show up in shyness, silence, long speeches, super-rationality, coolness, politeness, boasting, stupid jokes, giggling, and many other strange behaviors. A person who is emotionally healthy will drop these masks as he or she gets more comfortable and builds more trust. But if your partner never lets the mask slip, that might be a danger sign.

Sometimes it takes time to tell the difference between a potential aggressor, someone who's out of practice, and someone whose confusion is so strong that it makes him or her play games. Even people who mean well can do a lot of harm if they can't figure out what they do or don't want. They won't mean to hurt you, but that won't make it hurt any less if they do.

The art of self-protection includes the art of staying safe and keeping the question open while the layers of insecurity and confusion are peeled away. Underneath may be a rose or a thorn, a jewel or a jagged rock.

Notes

1. Several books in the Bibliography address effective ways of relating to others. One book that focuses specifically on accepting differences in relationships is Hugh and Gayle Prather's *A Book for Couples*.
2. Many books in the Bibliography address communication skills. For a broad look at communication skills you might start with McKay, Davis, and Fanning's *Messages*. For communication techniques specifically for couples, you might try Terence T. Gorski's *Getting Love Right*, Hugh and Gayle Prather's *A Book for Couples*, or Harville Hendrix's *The Couples Companion*.

Journal Questions

1. Which kinds of messages are you most used to sending: passive, aggressive, passive/aggressive, or assertive? What are some examples of these?

2. Have you ever been on a first date where one or both partners gave a lot of highly personal information? How might that situation have been different if people were more careful in deciding what to say and not to say?

3. What has been your experience of alcohol or other drugs and sexual involvement? What might have happened differently if neither partner was drunk or high?

4. When you're dating, how do your own insecurities show up?

CHAPTER 9

The Stages of Sexual Involvement

All the communication skills in the world can fail us if we don't know what we're describing. It's time to look at sexual involvement itself and think about ways of understanding it, talking about it, and making clear decisions about it. If you ask a young couple in the heat of passion, they'll tell you that it just "happens." But it's hard to understand a big blur that starts with a smile and ends with everybody's clothes in a lump on the floor. So sexual involvement has been "mapped out" in four stages: (1) acknowledgment of attraction, (2) flirtation, (3) sensual involvement, and (4) sexual involvement.

Mapping the Stages

Because setting limits and drawing boundaries are important parts of healthy involvement, it's important to know the territory. The four stages described in this chapter can help in that process.

It's also important to spot different ways of passing over the territory. Many of us have been schooled in unhealthy ways of moving from stage to stage, based on the old model of relationship. Those ways are sometimes different for men and women, but they often hook together—as if they're locking us into the old model. Even if we mean well, it can lead to big problems for one or both partners.

163

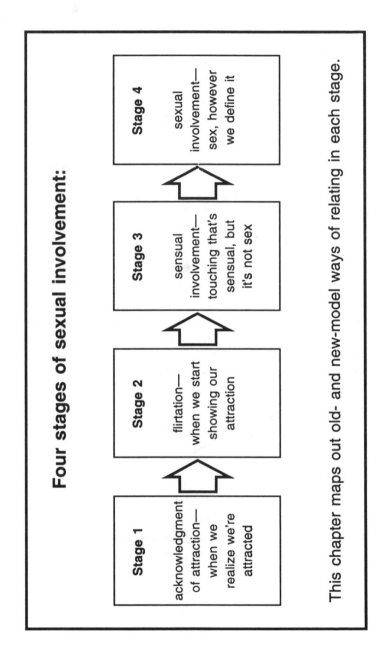

Four stages of sexual involvement:

Stage 1	Stage 2	Stage 3	Stage 4
acknowledgment of attraction— when we realize we're attracted	flirtation— when we start showing our attraction	sensual involvement— touching that's sensual, but it's not sex	sexual involvement— sex, however we define it

This chapter maps out old- and new-model ways of relating in each stage.

This chapter focuses on the unhealthy, old-model ways of traveling through these stages and the healthy ways that we use when we're following the new model of relationship. Before we look at the individual stages, it helps to look at some general differences between the ways we operate in the old and new models.

Movement from Stage to Stage

There are many choice points in the stages of sexual involvement. The most obvious ones are the boundaries between one stage and the next. That's why it's so important to understand healthy and unhealthy ways of moving from stage to stage.

In the new model, people move to the next stage carefully. Movement always waits for two things. The first is a request—verbal or nonverbal—from at least one partner. If that request isn't clear, the other partner uses words to ask what it means. Then the first partner uses words to clarify what he or she had in mind. Next, the other partner gives a "go" signal—verbal or nonverbal. If the "go" signal isn't clear, the first partner uses words to ask for a verbal okay. Unless both of those messages are clear, people stay in the current stage or back up into an earlier stage.

> **Often two people have been trained to communicate in different ways, and each one is expecting the other to read his or her mind.**

Each of these steps is the result of a choice one or both partners make. In the new model, both people are aware that they're making choices. They see each boundary between the stages as a choice point and they see themselves as choice makers.

In the old model, signals from either or both partners might not be clear—and even clear signals might not be respected. There are many ways this happens.

- One partner might try to move from stage to stage without making a clear request or getting a "go" signal from the other.
- One partner might send out a "stop" signal and the other might ignore it.
- One partner might make a request, but the other might ignore the request, hoping that the first partner will "get the message" that he or she isn't interested. Unfortunately, an aggressive partner is more likely to take a lack of reaction as a "go" signal.

Often the two partners have been trained to communicate in different ways, and each one is expecting the other to read his or her mind.

Honesty

In the new model of relationship, both verbal and nonverbal messages are honest. That means that the messages match what people really think, feel, want, and mean to say. Communication in the new model is clearer and better defined. In the old model it's usually a little fuzzy or confused.

In the old model, both verbal and nonverbal messages can be disguised or distorted. One or both partners might have hidden motives and try to trick the other. A manipulative or aggressive partner might not care about what the other partner wants, but only care about what *he or she* wants. Or the other partner might distort the messages by noticing danger signs and ignoring them—saying "I'm imagining things." Either partner might try to control the other or put the other off balance by giving mixed signals.

166

Dignity and Well-Being

In the new model both people tend to move slowly, whether or not they feel like it. They know it's best for both of them and for the relationship. Both people have a better chance of staying safely "centered" and in control of their own actions. That helps them move toward the dignity that's the cornerstone of the new model. In the old model, people tend to move more quickly. It's much easier for one or both people to lose their balance and control. It's much easier to make disastrous mistakes.

In the new model of relationship, people care about one another's well-being. Their good will doesn't depend on how well they know one another or what they think they can get from one another. In the old model, somebody's usually using someone else. People in the new model tend to see one another as equals. In the old model, it often turns into a "one-up/one-down" situation.

Your Effect on the Relationship

If someone you're dating tends to make the old-model mistakes described below, that might be a sign of manipulation or aggression. On the other hand, it might be a sign that he or she just lacks knowledge and skills. Or your partner might have the best skills but get carried away and "forget" to use them this time.

In the new model both people move slowly, whether or not they feel like it. They know it's best for both of them and for the relationship.

What's most important is that *you* have the knowledge and skills, and that *you* use them. In most cases, a partner who's determined to do it the right way can have a strong effect on the way the relationship develops. Often you can slow things down by going slowly and by setting—and protecting—clear limits. You can raise the level of mutual respect and well-being in the relationship by being respectful—and promoting each person's well being—with all your words and actions.

If your partner is willing to step into the new model with you, congratulations. You've made a step in your own growth and helped someone else grow at the same time. If your partner stays in the old model, you have some important information. He or she might be dangerous to you, or might just not be ready to relate in a healthy way. Acting on that information can save valuable time and energy that would be better spent on the next partner. It might even save your life.

Here are some new- and old-model ways of navigating the four stages.

Stage One: Acknowledgment of Attraction

This stage begins when one person first "notices" another—mentally separates him or her from the crowd and thinks, "Hmmm. . . I wonder. . .." It's a personal experience that takes place within an individual human being. Sometimes two people reach that realization about one another at the same time. But often one person reaches it alone. And the other has no idea, or notices it but doesn't feel the same.

In this stage the person who's attracted acknowledges the attraction to him- or herself. The stage ends when he or she expresses it, in verbal or nonverbal ways.

Acknowledgment of Attraction in the New Model

People with healthy relationship skills know they're going to be attracted to many people and realize they have a choice of whether or not to act on—or even show—that attraction. They don't deny to themselves that they're attracted. They just don't assign too much importance to it until they've thought it through. They know there's nothing wrong with being attracted to someone who's not attracted to them.

They mentally review the reasons it might or might not make sense to follow up on the attraction. Is the person married, engaged, going steady, or single? Does the person seem emotionally stable? Does he or she treat people well? Does this person produce feelings of comfort or feelings of anxiety?

Acknowledgment of Attraction

- New model— we're honest with ourselves, but we can choose whether or not to act on the attraction, and we take our time.
- Old model—we might be ashamed of our attraction and lie to ourselves, or think we have no choice but to get involved.

When Jeff was introduced to Kimberly, his new lab partner, bells and whistles went off in his head. He was so strongly attracted to her that even dead frogs seemed interesting when she was in the room. He decided to keep the attraction to himself for a while and stick to business. After a couple of weeks he realized he'd felt the same intense attraction to the last two women he'd dated. They'd turned out to be game players, and really worked him over emotionally.

He started noticing things Kimberly said and did that would annoy him or feel insulting if he weren't so strongly attracted.

169

She started reminding him more and more of the two women who'd worked him over—and even reminded him a little bit of his mother. He decided not to ask her out. It would be much better to fantasize about "the one that got away" than to deal with another broken heart and wounded ego.

Men and women with healthy relationship skills know that they're free not to follow up on their attraction. Even if the people they're attracted to are flirting like crazy, they can choose to act as if nothing sexual is going on. If they do decide to act on the attraction, it's a conscious, deliberate decision. They pick the right time, the right place, and the right way to start showing their attraction.

Acknowledgment of Attraction in the Old Model

In the old model, many people have trouble with this stage of involvement. Some feel ashamed of being attracted. They might think they're basically unattractive, so they fear rejection. Or they might have been taught to believe that desire is bad and shameful. As a result, they might feel awkward around people who attract them, or they might treat those people in unfriendly ways.

To escape those uncomfortable feelings, some people convince themselves that they're not really attracted. That's more dangerous, because then they become unaware of any sexual signals they may be giving off, and they miss important signals that others might be sending. For example, Louise was attracted to Brian, but she told herself she wasn't. He was picking up subtle signs of attraction from her, but she wasn't aware she was sending any signs. And because she told herself there was nothing sexual between them, she didn't pay attention to the signs of attraction he was sending. She didn't let him know that she wasn't interested.

She ended up alone with him on a deserted beach, where he made his first moves. She was shocked. When she slapped him, he was shocked, too. Fortunately, Brian wasn't a rapist. But there are still some hurt feelings between them.

Safety in Acknowledgment of Attraction

- Be aware when you're attracted to someone—and when you aren't.
- Don't be ashamed of being attracted.
- Get to know people first on a nonsexual basis.
- Save the attraction until it's safe to show it.
- Ask yourself how far you're willing to go at this time.

Many people believe that if they're attracted to someone they have no choice but to show that attraction—whether or not they want to act on it. They tend to show their attraction too early. They don't give themselves a chance to think about it, to decide if they really want to get to know this person or go out with him or her. They often raise people's social or sexual expectations. By acting on the attraction too soon, they start a series of events that's harder and harder to get out of as it progresses.

Safety Measures in Acknowledgment of Attraction

In this stage the most important safety measure is self-knowledge. It's important to know when you're attracted to someone. Attraction is nothing to be ashamed about, whether or not the other person is attracted to you. But you have to be the one to decide whether or not you're going to show that attraction or follow up on it.

You can always get to know someone on a nonsexual basis even if you're attracted to him or her. It's not dishonest to do that. You can save the attraction until you're sure it's safe to show it. Don't deny it to yourself—just don't start flirting yet. If you're both attracted, the attraction will keep. If it disappears, you can be sure it wouldn't have lasted long anyway.

If you do decide to show your attraction now, please know that it will advance you into the flirting stage. Once you're there, you won't always know how your signals are being interpreted. Before you start showing your attraction, ask yourself how far you're willing to go at this time. Be prepared to tell the other person clearly what your desires or intentions are, and what your limits are. If you don't know, be prepared to say that you don't know—or wait until you do know.

Stage Two: Flirting

In the flirting stage the sexual communication is often nonverbal. One person "lights up" when another enters the room. Each person might seem to find what the other is saying far more fascinating than it really is. Or they might lock eyes a moment too long, or smile and laugh when nothing's really *that* funny. Verbal messages might include compliments or mentioning that they're interested in the same kinds of things. The closest thing to a direct verbal message might be to ask for a date.

This stage begins when one or both people start to show their attraction. Then it includes all the subtle ways people continue to show attraction. Meanwhile each one is trying to figure out if the other is attracted, too, and deciding whether or not to get further involved. Sometimes the people are dating during this stage, or still "dancing around" one another in work, school, or social situations. This stage ends when physical contact begins.

```
┌─────────────────────────────────────────────┐
│                  Flirting                     │
│                                               │
│   • New model—flirting builds slowly, with    │
│     clear communication.                      │
│   • Old model—we move quickly, and we might   │
│     be dishonest and use flirting as a tool   │
│     for manipulation.                         │
│                                               │
└─────────────────────────────────────────────┘
```

Flirting in the New Model

In the new model of relationship, the flirting stage is a dance that builds slowly. It often begins with small signs of attraction that feel safe to the people involved. They might wait to see if the attraction is returned, then move to verbal messages. If one person isn't sure whether or not the other is flirting, he or she might even ask. If the answer is yes and both people seem pleased with it, they know it's okay for the flirting to continue.

If only one person is attracted, the other can also send a verbal or nonverbal "stop" signal. One nonverbal signal might be to choose not to respond to the other partner's nonverbal messages. The partner who's not interested might just act more distant or businesslike. Karla has a technique that she calls "icing." She's a strikingly attractive woman who is often on the receiving end of flirting from men she doesn't know. Icing is a look she gives them. It stops the flirting cold. It's not an angry look or a disrespectful look. It just says, "Don't even bother."

If one person asks for a date and the other isn't interested, a healthy stop signal would be to say no. Simply putting the person off by saying, "Oh, gee. I'm busy this Friday," won't do it, though. Putting people off like this might appear to be a kind way of letting them down easily. It isn't. When we put people off, we fail to give them important information they need to decide how to relate to us. An effective "no" will gently make it clear that it isn't just "no" for this Friday: It's "no" in general.

In the new model, the flirting stage might progress over a long time. This gives both people a chance to find out if they really like one another, trust one another, and enjoy spending time together. The sexual attraction can be intense, and it can be hard to wait before moving to the next stage. It pays to wait, though, for many reasons. As time goes on, they'll see one another more clearly. They can compare their current experience with past experiences they've had, to see if they're following any destructive patterns.

If they wait, they'll make better decisions about whether or not to get involved. They'll also be better friends by the time they make those decisions. And if the attraction and desire keep growing stronger while they wait, what's wrong with that?

If one person wants to stop being involved at this stage, that person stops flirting or dating and finds a way to explain clearly and respectfully that he or she doesn't want to stay involved. People with healthy relationship skills understand that disappointing people isn't the same thing as hurting them. And the person who wanted to stay involved knows it's okay to be disappointed and to express that disappointment honestly.

Flirting in the Old Model

In the old model of relationship, flirting is often used as a tool to manipulate others. And, of course, manipulation works best if the process is going on while the other partner isn't aware of it. People who use flirting in manipulation often don't like to admit they're flirting. If they admitted it, they'd have to take responsibility for their part in it. They'd rather make it all appear to be the other person's doing.

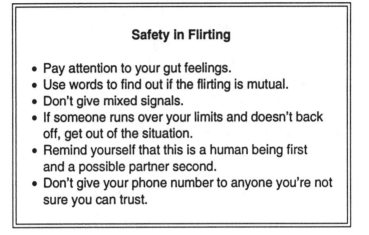

Safety in Flirting

- Pay attention to your gut feelings.
- Use words to find out if the flirting is mutual.
- Don't give mixed signals.
- If someone runs over your limits and doesn't back off, get out of the situation.
- Remind yourself that this is a human being first and a possible partner second.
- Don't give your phone number to anyone you're not sure you can trust.

Another problem in the old model is that flirting—and even things that aren't flirting—are often mistaken for sexual "go" signals. In a series of interviews with men, *New Woman* journalist Neil Chesanow heard men name a number of things that they found "seductive" when a woman did them. These included running her fingers through her hair, wearing attractive clothes, wearing perfume, making eye contact, making physical contact of any kind, or even swearing. Any of these are things a woman might do when there's no one around who attracts her. And even being attracted to someone isn't the same as wanting sex. In the old model all of these things get confused and jumbled together.[1]

Flirting can also be made out to be more important than it is. Someone who wants to trick a partner into greater involvement—either sexual or romantic—might choose to see the partner's flirtation as a sign of willingness or commitment.

175

"The chemistry between us is so strong, I just know this is meant to be!" The partner might have no idea that's how his or her actions are being taken until it's too late.

In the old model the flirting stage might not last too long. Unlike in the new model—where both people are using this stage to make up their minds slowly and carefully—someone who's using flirtation as a tool for manipulation has probably already made up his or her mind. This stage is just a way to get the other person into the next stage. The manipulative person doesn't want the other to have time to think and make a careful decision about getting involved.

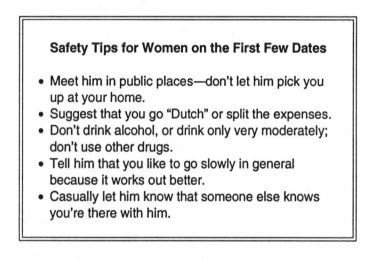

Safety Tips for Women on the First Few Dates

- Meet him in public places—don't let him pick you up at your home.
- Suggest that you go "Dutch" or split the expenses.
- Don't drink alcohol, or drink only very moderately; don't use other drugs.
- Tell him that you like to go slowly in general because it works out better.
- Casually let him know that someone else knows you're there with him.

Some people in the old model tend to get "obsessive" about potential partners. They "obsess"—think about the partner all the time, with stronger emotions than the situation calls for. Eventually they won't leave the partner alone, and won't stop trying to win him or her over. Sometimes they get very aggressive. If people have a tendency to get obsessive, this might be the stage where that tendency will start to show.

176

When the other partner starts sending "stop" or "slow down" signals, the obsessive partner will actually get more interested, more aggressive, and more obsessed. It's as if the obsessive partner is turned on by being rejected. These people sometimes become the "stalkers" who follow people home and park outside their houses at night. At the extreme end, they physically attack the people who are the objects of their obsession. Obsessive partners are very dangerous. Reasoning with them doesn't help. They continue to become more obsessive over time.

Safety Measures in the Flirting Stage

The first safety measure is to pay attention to your own "gut" feelings. If you don't feel good about something that someone is doing—or something you're doing in return—don't ignore that feeling. That holds true even if the person is acting right but there's something about him or her that doesn't feel right. You have a right to back out of a flirting situation at any time.

If you notice someone flirting and you *do* want to get involved in the flirting stage, it's best to put it in words. If you say, "Are you flirting with me?" in a welcoming tone of voice, it becomes part of the flirtation. If the answer is yes, you can always say something like "Good!" Then both people know where they stand. If the answer is no, that might mean the other person isn't interested, or it might mean that he or she is playing games. Either way, that's important information for you to have.

Again, there's nothing wrong with being attracted to people who aren't attracted to you. There's nothing wrong with being disappointed when they say no and expressing that disappointment honestly. As long as you do it directly and honestly—and don't try to push it or make them feel guilty—

you both get to keep your dignity. You might respond to the "no" with something like, "That's too bad. You'd be a wonderful person to flirt with. Let me know if you change your mind." Then stop flirting. If you get a "go" signal later, you can decide if you want to start again, or if you think the person is playing games.

If you set a limit and the other person steps over that limit and doesn't back off, that's a danger sign. If someone—male or female—gets more aggressive the more you try to back off, that's an even stronger sign of danger. This person might be obsessive. First, make sure you're not flirting a little bit and giving mixed signals. If you realize that you're giving mixed signals, stop doing it. Then make your plans to get away from the person—and certainly don't let yourself be caught alone with him or her. It's not easy to get out of an obsessive relationship at any stage, but it's much easier in the flirting stage. After sensual and sexual involvement have begun, it can be almost impossible.

If you're in the flirting stage with someone and you feel good about it, congratulations! Your job at this point is not to fight nature but to remind yourself—as often as possible— that this is a human being. Think as much as possible about who this person really is, apart from what you might want from him or her. Try to think of the person as a friend first and a potential partner second. And remember: Each partner has a right to choose when, where, and how to move to the next stage.

If you're a woman who's just starting to date a man, it's best not to have him pick you up at your home. Suggest that you meet at a restaurant or coffee shop—and stay there—or go out with friends. Don't say, "I'm afraid you might be a rapist." Put it positively: "I'd rather meet you there. I find that things work out better if I go slowly." It's also a good idea to suggest going "Dutch" or splitting the expenses. If possible, don't drink alcoholic beverages. If you can't avoid it, drink only moderately. And avoid using other drugs, especially if he's providing them. It's also a good idea to say something casually in conversation that lets him know you've told someone else where you'll be and that you'll be with him. It's not paranoid to be careful. Many women have been raped by men who appeared to be very safe and respectable.

Stage Three: Sensual Involvement

This stage is a little complicated because its beginning and ending points aren't always easy to pin down. Sensual involvement is physical contact that's meant to be sexually arousing—but it still isn't sex. So, for example, some hugs—and even some kisses—are sensual, and some aren't. It depends on who's doing it, how they're doing it, and why they're doing it. Our bodies are programmed to tell the difference. We just need to program our brains to listen to what our bodies are saying.

The end point of sensual involvement—the place where it turns into sexual involvement—is hard to define because different people see that limit at different places. One of the authors (Terry) once taught a college course in Statistics and Sexuality. He gave the students a long list of sensual or sexual acts. He asked them to check each one they'd ever done with a partner. For each one they checked, they were asked to answer this question: "In your mind, would you consider that you had sex when you did this?"

Terry expected most students to answer the questions in the same ways. They didn't. There were big differences among their answers. One student considered that she'd "had sex" when she "French-kissed" someone. And a number of students—most of them women—didn't consider having oral sex to be "having sex."

The legal boundary between sensual and sexual touching is at "genital stimulation." But someone's psychological boundary line might be almost anywhere. So it's possible to be having sex—at least in the other person's experience—and not even know it.

Sensual Involvement in the New Model

In the new model, both people start out knowing where they—as individuals—believe the sensual involvement stage begins and ends. They also start out knowing their own individual desires and limits. They're willing to talk about what they think, feel, believe, want, and don't want. And they care about what their partners think, feel, believe, want, and don't want.

Sensual touching is often used as a tool in seduction. Both partners know that desire can make it easy for people to ignore their responsibilities as friends—and as friends to themselves. They're willing to put in extra effort to make sure that doesn't happen. They know there are many choice points in this stage—points where both partners need to think about what's happening and decide whether they want it to go any further.

They also know that at those choice points it's important to put their thoughts, feelings, desires, and limits into words.

In the new model, both people understand that "yes" means "yes" and "no" means "no." The partner who starts the sensual touching does so carefully. This is to make sure the other partner really wants to be in this stage. Checking it out verbally doesn't have to be a clumsy process that spoils the mood. The words can become part of the sensual involvement. Instead of, "Is it okay if I put my hand there?" he or she might say something like, "Would you like me to touch you there?" The use of the right words and the right tone of voice can actually make the experience more erotic.

Both people take responsibility for clear communication about whether or not it's okay to move into further involvement. If one partner wants to stop or wait, the other stops or waits until the first partner says it's okay to proceed further. Both partners know that people take different lengths of time to know whether they want to get further involved, and to feel safe enough to take the next step. They also know that people have a right to change their minds and stop the process at any time.

Sensual Involvement in the Old Model

In the old model, one partner might "plow ahead" into and through this stage without making a clear request or waiting for "go" signals from the other. The partner who's starting the touching might even ignore the other partner's "stop" signals. Like the first two stages, this one tends to build quickly in the old model. Most aggressive and manipulative people don't want to give their partners a chance to stop the action. Many also believe—or pretend they believe—that "no" means "yes." And many well-meaning people don't understand the value of taking this stage slowly.

Sometimes even if one partner doesn't want the sensual touching, he or she might go along with it. This is always a mistake. Any sensual or sexual activity can be harmful if it takes place against someone's wishes. But partners aren't mind readers. They can't tell that their actions aren't wanted unless they get clear "stop" signals. And nonverbal stop signals are unreliable. It's easy to misunderstand them—or to miss them completely.

Beth is a survivor of childhood sexual abuse. She has a lot of conflicts about sensual and sexual issues. When she and Larry were taking a walk on their first date, he put his arm around her and began rubbing her shoulders in a sensual way. Even though she liked Larry, she didn't want to be sexual with him. She felt suddenly sick and panicky. She didn't say anything, though. She just got quiet and walked more stiffly. Larry didn't notice. When they reached her car, he kissed her sensually on the mouth. Again, she did nothing to stop him. She just retreated further inside her own mind. She drove home feeling shaken, traumatized, betrayed, and very angry.

It's in the sensual involvement stage that some situations head toward disaster. People have so many different beliefs about sensual touching. Some see it as a way of being emotionally intimate. Others see it as a promise of sex. Many more people are confused about what it means. It's possible for two people to be acting in good faith—but out of different belief systems—and end up with one or both people feeling used, frustrated, attacked, and unfairly accused. That's why words are so important from the beginning.

People who are manipulative or aggressive often use their partners' confusion about sensual touching to their own advantage. Take the example of a man who doesn't put his intentions into words but plows on ahead into sensual touching. The woman might want the sensual touching, but not want to go any further. She might or might not say so. Depending on his psychological makeup, the man might eventually talk her into having sex, or even rape her. He could tell her—and himself—that the sensual touching has taken him "past the point of no return."

Of course, there is no "point of no return." No man is forced by biology or circumstances to rape a woman. But some men haven't had the kinds of training that would help them learn to control their actions and take responsibility for what they do. That doesn't mean they're not responsible for their actions and for the effects of these actions. But women need to know that there are men who are able to talk themselves into rape, especially if they've been involved in sensual touching. No matter how good the sensual touching might feel, it's not worth the risk of rape.

Another example of manipulation in this stage is a woman who uses flirtation or sensual touching to turn a man on, but who really wants to get him excited and then stop him. This case is quite different from that of the woman who's just confused or who doesn't know how to set clear limits. This woman knows exactly what she's doing and why. She's playing a game in order to feel powerful and attractive. The fact that a few women play these kinds of games is often used against the many who don't. It's used as an excuse for taking advantage of women who simply don't know how to set clear limits.

Safety Measures in Sensual Involvement

At this stage the most important safety measure is clear communication. That includes being honest and open—at each choice point—about what you want and don't want. It also includes paying attention to the verbal and nonverbal messages your partner is sending—and being willing to ask for clarification even if it feels awkward.

If you see danger signs, don't analyze or rationalize them. Get safe. Make sure you don't get put in a position where you're alone with the person unless you're absolutely sure he or she isn't going to take advantage of you. You have a right to decide where to go on a date. You also have a right to end the date at any point—even halfway through the salad course.

Before the sensual touching begins, decide how far you want to go this time. Kissing and hugging? Hands outside the clothes? Petting above the waist? Talk to your partner about your limits, and listen to what he or she is saying. If it sounds as if your partner is agreeing just to get you to shut up, beware. Above all, listen to your "gut" feelings about this person and the way the date is going. If you don't feel safe, don't be afraid to make your excuses and leave. It's also okay to leave with no warning and no explanation.

Safety in Sensual Involvement

- Know what sensual involvement means to you and how far you want to go.
- Be honest and open about your wants and limits from the start, using clear and direct words.
- Pay attention to verbal and nonverbal signals, and ask for clarification.
- Pay attention to your gut feelings; if you don't feel safe, get out.
- If you're not friends yet, think about letting this stage wait.
- Know that you can control your own actions, even if you're turned on.
- Even if your partner says "I can't stop," don't do anything you don't want to do or you don't feel good about.

Even in the new model of relationship, the time spent in passionate kissing and petting makes it very difficult not to zoom into the next stage before you're both sure it's a good idea. It also pulls energy and attention away from the developing friendship. Unless you're already true friends—and you're pretty sure you want to get fully involved—it might be better to stay in the flirting stage for a while and let this stage wait.

Stage Four: Sexual Involvement

This is the final stage. It begins when people progress to sexual touching—whatever they define that to be.

Sexual Involvement in the New Model

In the new model of relationship, both partners think hard and communicate well before they decide whether or not to enter this stage. First they compare notes to see where each partner believes this stage begins. Often it's not the same for both partners. If that's the case, it's important for them to know. They need to talk about and make a decision on what they will and won't do.

A man in the new model knows that the risk of rape and manipulation is too high to let him assume the woman wants whatever he wants. He takes responsibility for asking her in clear, understandable terms. A woman knows that even well-meaning men can't read her mind. She takes responsibility for making her wishes and limits clear, using direct words.

Both partners know about the risk of getting HIV, the virus that causes AIDS, or other sexually transmitted diseases. That risk is too high not to talk about—and use—latex condoms treated with the spermicide Nonoxynol-9. If one or both partners are in their teens, they understand that they probably aren't emotionally ready for sex—even though they might feel physically ready. They can help one another wait.

Sexual Involvement

- New model—we know and communicate well about what we want, what our partner wants, and how we're going to protect ourselves and one another.
- Old model—we only care what *we* want, or we get forced or manipulated into doing what we don't want; we don't worry about disease or pregnancy.

If one or both partners are emotionally vulnerable—in early sobriety, for example, or going through severe depression—they know that sex at this time could put them in emotional danger. They help one another wait. In the new model, people do what's best for them in the long term—not just what feels good now.

Sexual Involvement in the Old Model

In the old model, it's all about instant gratification. People sometimes enter this stage against the will of one partner. This can happen deliberately, as in the case of rape or manipulation. It can also happen by accident, if both people fail to communicate well.

Sometimes people enter this stage willingly, but before they're prepared. They might be too young or emotionally vulnerable. They might not know one another well enough, so they become physically intimate before they're ready to trust one another. Or they might not have the right protection against disease and unwanted pregnancy.

Safety Measures in Sexual Involvement

As in the sensual involvement stage, the most important safety measure is clear communication. You both need to take full responsibility for making sure you understand one another's wishes and limits clearly. Knowing yourself—what you really want and how vulnerable you are—is critical at this stage.

Again, if you've decided to have sex, a latex condom with Nonoxynol-9 is the most important safety measure. Even if you use other forms of birth control, they won't protect against the spread of HIV and other infections. You might be afraid to bring up these subjects because you don't want to spoil the mood. Bring them up anyway. If the mood is so fragile that honest communication will ruin it, then it's meant to be broken. That might be a sign that both partners aren't ready.

Safety in Sexual Involvement

- Make sure you know what sexual involvement means to you and what you want and don't want.
- Communicate these things clearly to your partner, and ask him or her to communicate clearly with you about these things.
- Listen to your partner's desires and limits.
- Respect all limits—yours and your partner's.
- If you do have sex, use a latex condom with Nonoxynol-9 to protect against the spread of HIV and other infections.

If one partner tries to manipulate the other into having sex, the best safety measures are a clear knowledge of rights and limits, and assertive communication skills. If a man is willing to rape, his partner will need an escape route, and/or skills in self-defense. The following chapter gives a few tips on handling manipulation and the threat of rape. But there's no substitute for skills in physical self-defense. And the best defense against all of these problems is to avoid being alone with someone until he or she has earned your trust.

Healthy Sexuality in the New Model

There's nothing wrong with desire or the satisfaction of desire. It's using people that causes problems. It's rape and manipulation that are destructive.

Part of our legacy of confusing sex with aggression is that many of us still have some funny ideas about sex. Some still think sex is dirty and shameful. Others think it's a way to prove themselves or to solve their problems. Some think it's a way to get close to someone who can't seem to get close any other way. It's none of those things, though. It's just sex. It will always take its value from the quality of the communication, compatibility, and friendship between two people.

Not everyone needs deeper love and commitment to have healthy sexual involvement. Many people do, but others don't. They just need mutual respect. Some people go through phases. They'll start out just wanting sex for enjoyment, but wake up one morning knowing that's no longer enough for them.

Sex is just sex. It doesn't prove our worth or make people love us. It's as good or bad as our communication, compatibility, and friendship.

What matters is that people are honest with one another—and with themselves—about what it means to them. You can pass through the stages slowly. You can get all your "stop" and "go" signals right. You can use just the right condom. But if one person thinks it's love and the other thinks it's just sex, it *will* be destructive. You can count on it.

In the new model, sexuality and eroticism—sexual desire and pleasure—are lifted out of their old, violent frame.

Healthy sexuality doesn't depend on the thrill of danger. It recognizes the more subtle sensations, like the thrill of having the courage to be honest. It doesn't rush toward its goal. It takes its time. If the desire keeps building in intensity, so much the better. The process itself is the goal—the slow building of intimacy and pleasure.

In the new model, people don't avoid being honest about what they want, out of a fear of spoiling the mystery. They understand that human beings are by nature mysterious. No amount of honest communication can spoil that. Nothing they can say about their desires and limits can even scratch the surface of who they are.

The beauty of desire can't be spoiled by friendship. It can only grow deeper and stronger.

Notes

1. See Neil Chesanow's "Sex, Lies, and Dating: What's Really on His Mind?" in *New Woman* (August 1994).

Journal Questions

1. Have you ever thought someone was attracted to you who wasn't—or failed to notice when someone was attracted to you? What signals did you miss or misinterpret?

2. What do you think is the best way of letting someone know you don't want to get involved? What would your reactions be if someone used that method to let you know *they* didn't want to get involved?

3. In your experience, does it get harder to slow down or stop involvement the farther you go? Has there been a particular point where it starts to get much more difficult to stop—or to stop the other person?

4. Deep down, what do you really believe about sex? Does it get mixed up in your mind with other things, like violence, security, or power? What do you believe it will do for you, or for the other person?

5. In dating, what are some "choice points" along the way—places where you might increase your safety?

PART V

Sexual Force
and
Manipulation

CHAPTER 10

The Continuum of Sexual Aggression

This chapter takes a closer look at some of the ways sexual aggression takes place. Laying all these behaviors out in a line isn't meant to exaggerate the importance of the least violent behaviors. And it certainly isn't meant to underplay the horrors of the most violent. It's just meant to help make sense of something that many of us find confusing.

Making sense of something isn't the same as excusing it or saying it's "just part of human nature." Rape is so much against our nature as human beings that many people believe it doesn't deserve to be understood. But as long as a lack of understanding puts people at greater risk, we can't afford *not* to make sense of it. We all deserve to live in a society that can understand—and overcome—sexual manipulation and force.

This chapter might be hard to read. It deals with some unpleasant things that happen between people. It also talks about mistakes that some men make, and mistakes that some women make. No mistake on a woman's part can make her responsible for being raped, or excuse the rapist's actions. But women who make high-risk choices need to understand and replace those choices. If they don't, they'll continue to be far too vulnerable to sexual force and manipulation.

The Continuum of Sexual Aggression

Healthy Sexuality:
- Sexual assertiveness—honest and open expression of desire

Manipulation:
- Seduction—using sensual desire and pleasure to break through resistance
- Psychological force—using a threat to self-esteem to get sex

Rape:
- Threat of physical force—threatening the partner's safety or freedom to get sex
- Physical force—sex by physical force, against the partner's wishes

The Continuum of Aggression

"Continuum" is a useful word. It's an imaginary line that stretches from one end of human experience to the opposite end. Points or stages along that line show a slow, steady increase in certain conditions. In this case, the continuum of sexual aggression runs from sexual assertiveness to physical force. The points on this continuum, from the low end to the high end, are sexual assertiveness, seduction, psychological force, threat of physical force, and physical force.

The first of these points, sexual assertiveness, is the only healthy spot on the continuum. The second and third points, seduction and psychological force, are types of manipulation. The last two points, threat of physical force and physical force, are types of rape. All of these categories are explained in the following pages.

Most people don't just get stuck at one point along this continuum and stay there. People move back and forth in the course of their lives—and sometimes in the course of a single date. Someone might be falling into more and more dangerous patterns, and so move more toward the aggressive end of the continuum. Someone else might be learning and growing and getting healthier, and so move back toward the less aggressive end. Some people move back and forth on purpose, in order to get more power over others. Each time we move, it takes a choice on our part, whether or not we're aware that we're making a choice.

Remember Don and Sandy from Part II? Possible events in their evening will be used to show the points on this continuum. Although in these examples Don is usually the aggressive one, there are also some examples of women manipulating men. But because women face more physical danger from sexual aggression, the chapter focuses more on men's use of force and manipulation.

Sexual Assertiveness

Sexual assertiveness is an honest, straightforward expression of desire. No tricks are used, and no unfair pressure is applied. It's an honorable process that takes place between people who consider themselves equals. It fits in well with the new model.

When Don is dropping Sandy off at home, they begin to kiss in the car. At some point he asks her if he can come in for a while. "I'll be honest," he might say. "I'm really attracted to you, and I think we should make love." If Sandy says no, he might say, "That's too bad. I think we'd have a wonderful time. So do you mean, 'No, not tonight,' 'No, not with you,' or 'No, I'm not ready to decide'?"

In Sexual Assertiveness

- We're honest, open, and straightforward about our desire.
- We don't use tricks or pressure.
- It's an honorable process between equals.
- We're willing to wait.
- We know we can control our actions.
- We find out whether or not we should ask again.
- We decide whether or not we really want to get to know this person.
- We continue to negotiate and renegotiate limits with our partner.

Don's willingness to be honest has given Sandy a chance to draw the line. He's been clear about his desires and honest about his disappointment when she said no. He hasn't begged, though, and he hasn't tried to use tricks or force. Both people have kept their dignity.

Don knows he can control his actions, even though he'd rather not. He's willing to wait until he can have sex with someone who really wants to have sex with him. That person might be Sandy at a later date, or it might be someone else. He's asking for more information, so he'll know whether or not to bring up the question in the future.

Next, Don has to decide whether or not he really wants to get to know Sandy. He asks himself, "If I knew she'd never want to have sex with me, would I still want to get to know her and be her friend?" If the answer is no, then he knows it's just as well that they didn't have sex this time. If he doesn't value her highly enough to want to get to know her for herself, then sex probably wouldn't be healthy for either of them. He knows that if he continues to see her just on the hope of having sex, it won't be a healthy relationship. Both partners stand a good chance of feeling used.

If both people really want to get to know one another, though, they can begin to build a friendship. Don walks her to her door but doesn't try to talk or force his way inside. He doesn't try to make her feel guilty. He lets her know he'd like to see her again. As they get to know one another, they work together on setting—and re-setting—boundaries and limits that are comfortable for both. Neither one of them violates those boundaries or plays games.

As you can imagine, this way of relating to one another takes skill, self-knowledge, patience, respect, and careful thought. If Don and Sandy had been drinking too much or using other drugs, they might not have been able to stay within the boundaries of sexual assertiveness.

Seduction

Seduction might be thought of as "soft-core manipulation." It moves beyond sexual assertiveness into the area of dishonesty and aggression. In its original meaning, "to seduce" meant "to lead away." In seduction one partner tries to lead the other away from the needs and realities of his or her life. The aggressive partner uses sensual desire and pleasure as a drug to put the other partner's defenses to sleep. On an emotional level, seduction is almost a hypnotic process.

Both partners are preoccupied with the growing sexual feelings. They lose contact with real life. The seducer's fantasy is that none of this will have any effect on the rest of reality. That fantasy is shared with the person being seduced. But particularly if the seducer is a man, he also begins at this point to separate his actions from their consequences. In a way, he's getting prepared to become more aggressive later.

Let's say Don wants to seduce Sandy. He uses their kissing

and petting in his car as a way of raising her desire and lowering her resistance. He doesn't say what he wants. Instead, he wants her to focus on what's happening in that moment and how good it feels. He might speak in romantic words and play soft music on the radio. When he asks her to invite him inside her apartment, he says it's because they can be more comfortable there. He might even have some drugs he'd like to share with her when they get inside.

In Seduction

- We "hypnotize" our partner with desire and pleasure.
- We distract our partner from the realities of life.
- We separate our actions from their consequences.
- We might not be aware that we're being seduced.

Don knows he's trying to seduce her, but he sees that process as a normal, healthy part of being a man. After all, he's been watching TV and movies all his life. He's been trained to believe that seduction is an important part of sex. Using the more direct techniques described above under "sexual assertiveness" would seem crazy to him. That would make it easier for her to say no! He's been trained to believe that this is a game and that it's his job to win it.

Sandy might or might not try to stop him, because she might or might not be aware that she's being seduced. She might start out with a clear decision not to have sex with him on the first date but get more and more confused about that as the evening wears on. She might forget her arguments against it, including the very real concerns she'd wake up with the next morning. Instead, she just feels flattered by his attention. She feels special.

The problem with seduction is that it's a very subtle, very sneaky way of getting around someone's true wishes. Sandy might not be emotionally ready to have sex with Don—or with anyone—tonight. She might want to get to know him better, to decide whether she wants to be physically intimate with him. She might need more time to find out if he's emotionally stable. Either one of them might be in a committed relationship with someone else. She might not have the right kind of birth control, or they might not have the right kind of condom for protection against HIV/AIDS.

Because Don's tactics are so smooth, Sandy might feel as if stating those concerns would make her sound too clumsy. If she has low skills in communication, self-confidence, and limit setting, she might not know how to express her concerns clearly. If she has a low sense of self-worth, she might feel she has no right to refuse him. She's also heard all those cultural messages that say a woman "owes a man something" if he spends time with her and pays for the drinks, drugs, and dinner.

If Sandy's sure she wants to go to bed with Don tonight, then there's no problem. But if Don seduces Sandy into having sex with him, she'll probably feel betrayed—by Don and by herself. She's also been betrayed by the popular culture, though. That culture trained her to be seduced, to feel ashamed of it, and to blame herself. The sex might not have been forced, but it wasn't freely chosen. Don might not have lied, but he didn't respect her wishes enough to find out what they really were.

When Men Are Seduced

Some women seduce men, too. If our culture winks when a woman is seduced by a man, then it gives a great big grin when a man is seduced by a woman. Men are less likely to feel shame and self-blame when they've been seduced, but men can also be hurt by seduction. Our culture doesn't often admit it, but men are sexually vulnerable and need emotional intimacy. Many men have sexual standards, boundaries, and limits, too. They suffer if those things aren't respected.

As mentioned in the last chapter, some women play "tease" games. They act very seductive and give many "go" signals, but then refuse to have sex. Usually this is a way of trying to feel more attractive and powerful. If a woman who's playing this game happens to be in the company of a man who has a tendency to rape, then she's likely to be raped. She won't *deserve* to be raped, but that won't stop the man from doing it. If a woman appears to be playing this game, her partner needs to remember four things:

1. Rape is rape, no matter what the woman has said or done. The effects of rape are always serious. It's never worth it.

2. Raping this woman wouldn't "teach" her anything. All it would do would be to hurt her and yourself. If you really want to help her stop playing these games, then talk to her about what she's doing. But don't get drawn back into the game.

3. Most women don't play these games. You don't need someone who does.

4. You don't have to force yourself on anyone. You can choose to respect yourself more than that.

One important note: The fact that a few women play seduction games doesn't mean that all women who pull back during seduction are playing games. For many women, a man's seductive process works like a powerful drug. They might go along with it for a while, then "wake up" and realize that they really don't want to have sex—or realize for the first time that the man expects sex. Those decisions should always be respected.

If this happens, some men might feel that their dignity and self-respect are being threatened by the woman's refusal to go any further. A man can save his dignity at this point by stopping the seductive moves and switching to a less sexual kind of communication. But then it's important that he doesn't let himself get drawn into the seductive mode again.

Breaking the Power of Seduction

Seduction gets most of its power from secrecy and from something that might be called "emotional logic." This logic says, "If it feels good, do it, and don't think about it." The secrecy of seduction keeps the seduced partner from checking with others to see if what's going on really makes sense. Seduction invites both partners to focus on their sexual feelings and turn off their minds and their intuitive sense that something is wrong. It's a game where direct words aren't allowed.

The best way to break through the seductive game is to break the no-talk rules. Say what you're feeling. Say what you think is happening. Say what you really want and don't want. Say that the evening's over when it's gone far enough. Don't worry if it sounds clumsy. You don't have to play by the rules of seduction. You can set new rules.

201

Psychological Force

Psychological force is "hard-core manipulation" that's based on a threat to self-esteem. Most people—men and women—have been well trained in manipulation all their lives. Since early childhood they've seen people use manipulative tools—things like guilt, sympathy, embarrassment, and the threat of the loss of love—to get what they want. Many people are better trained in manipulation than in direct communication. It's no wonder that these tools are so often used in getting sex.

Examples of Psychological Force

- I'm sad and lonely and sex will help me.
- This could be love; don't blow it by saying no.
- I'm in no shape to drive; can I stay here?
- I promise I won't try anything.
- You're just a tease.
- If you're truly liberated you'll have sex with me.
- If you don't, I'll tell everybody you did.
- It's gone too far; I can't stop.

The use of psychological force to get sex has also become a big part of the image of the "real man." There's so much cultural approval of sexual manipulation that many men don't see it as manipulation—or they think manipulation is healthy and "normal." Many TV and movie legends—like Sam Malone of "Cheers" fame—have been built on seduction and psychological force.

If Don chooses to use psychological force on Sandy, he might begin by tricking her into being alone with him. He might tell her he really wants her to meet his roommate and his roommate's girlfriend—then make some excuse when they get to his apartment and find no one else there. Once they're alone, he'll start his seductive moves. As the seduction fails to work, he'll add psychological force.

He might decide to play on her sympathy: "I've been really lonely since Cathy left me. I'm beginning to feel like I'm closed off from the world, and nobody can ever get through to me." He's trying to convince her she'll be depriving him if she turns him down, turning down a chance to heal him. He might try to convince Sandy she'd be missing a chance for real love if she turned him down: "I haven't felt like this about anybody for so long. If you leave tonight, I feel like I'll never be able to trust you again. It's like we've stumbled onto something important, and if we don't take advantage of it now, we'll lose it."

On the other hand, he might decide to be more "practical" about it: "I'm in no shape to drive anymore tonight. Would you mind staying here, and I can run you home tomorrow? I promise I won't try anything." Or he might try to make her feel socially clumsy about refusing: "Come on. Don't tell me you have all those hang-ups! You seem smarter and more liberated than all that. I thought you were a woman! Don't tell me you're just a little girl!"

There's only one good reason to have sex with someone: Because you really want to have sex with this particular person, right now.

If they've been necking and petting for a while, Don might use the familiar "I can't stop" argument: "You've been leading me on all evening. You can't stop me now! Don't you know what it *does* to a man if a woman takes him this far and just shuts him down?" If he's willing to get nasty, he can threaten her reputation: "C'mon. If you stop me now I just might have to tell everybody what a little tease you are. Or maybe I'll have to tell them you threw yourself at me. It'll be your word against mine."[1]

If Sandy has a strong enough sense of self-esteem—and a good enough "B.S. detector"—she'll probably see through Don's manipulation. But if she's basically insecure, or feeling insecure because of events in her life, she might be fooled. She might be afraid of hurting him, losing his affection, or having her reputation damaged. She might believe she owes him sex because he's spent time and money on her.

She might believe that having sex with him will help her get rid of him. But chances are great that it won't. You can't remove a threat by giving in to it. You can only make it stronger.

Resisting Psychological Force

If you're caught up in word games with someone who wants to get you to bed, remember these four things:

1. There's only one good reason to have sex with someone: because you really want to have sex with this particular person, right now.

2. You're not responsible for anybody else's feelings, and you don't owe anyone an explanation of why you don't want sex. If you leave a partner feeling frustrated, he or she can always masturbate after you've parted company.

3. If someone will stop caring about you because you won't have sex, then he or she doesn't really care about you.

4. If you let someone blackmail you into sex this time, then it will probably happen again.

These guidelines hold true even if you've had sex with this partner before, and even if you're married to him or her. In many cultures there's a strong belief that one partner doesn't have a right to refuse sex if they're already "involved." The truth is that any woman, and any man, has a right to refuse any kind of sexual activity with anyone, at any time.

Many people who use psychological force believe that their sexual tactics come from desire, or from a desire for sexual freedom. But people really use psychological force because they're driven by fear. In this case it might be the fear of not meeting cultural standards, or the fear that they won't be able to find sexual partners any other way. It's not a desire for freedom that drives them, though: One person's freedom can't be bought by taking away any part of another person's freedom.

> **The truth is that any woman—and any man—has a right to refuse any kind of sexual activity with anyone, at any time.**

Common Excuses for Using Psychological Force

Men who want to justify their own use of psychological force often point to the fact that women use it on men, too. "If I don't trick her into bed, she'll just try to trick me into a committed relationship." This is where the commodity thinking blossoms. This is where the mistakes that some men and women make come together and create one big mistake. No form of manipulation can justify another form of manipulation. And as long as each side is waiting for the other to stop the manipulation first, the problems will continue forever.

Another rationalization some men use is: "She really wants me to go ahead and do it. If I just stop, she'll be disappointed and think I'm less of a man." But the truth is that she *doesn't* really want to be manipulated or forced into sex. And even if she is playing games, ask yourself: If a woman operates like that, do you want to have sex with her? Do you want to reward her games? Do you want to give her that kind of control over you?

If you're a man who's in the habit of using psychological force to get sex, it's important to remember four things:

1. There are other skills you can learn. You can find women who really want you as you are. You can get what you really need through honest communication.

2. If a woman turns you down, that doesn't make you any less of a man. All it means is that you won't have sex with this woman tonight.

3. Mature men don't want to have sex with people who don't want them. They respect women's wishes because they respect themselves and their integrity.

4. If a woman wants to have sex with you, she can let you know. It's not your job to read her mind or her mood. If you ask, she'll tell you. If she says no, it means no.

Threat of Physical Force

The threat of physical force takes it a step beyond manipulation, to rape. Here the partner's physical safety or freedom is threatened. If a woman can show that she was forced to have sex with a man because she believed he would hurt her or keep her from escaping, it fits the legal definition of rape. Sometimes it's called "coerced rape," because it's done with threats or "coercion."

If Don wanted to have sex with Sandy against her will, he might threaten her: "If you yell or try to fight back, you'll really regret it!" He might say that he has a weapon, or threaten to hit her if she tries to escape. If Sandy is physically weaker than Don, without skills in self-defense that would work against his strength, these threats can be terrifying. She may never find out if he would have carried out his threats. But for now, she knows he's physically capable of killing her or hurting her badly. That fear can be enough to paralyze her defenses.

Avoiding the Threat

Before the date begins, a woman needs to

- have an escape plan and self-defense plan ready and rehearsed;
- memorize the warning signs of rape (page 209);
- be willing to get out at the sign of threat; and
- convince herself that she's worth protecting.

Giving in to the Threat

Television and movies have carried many stories about women who were hurt or killed by rapists. This has made a strong impression in many women's minds. When a man threatens violence—even if he doesn't show any evidence of it—the images planted by those stories can make the man's threat seem very real.

But the media don't report the large number of attempted rapes that fail. Many women who have been attacked have fought back successfully and avoided being raped. Even so, the question for an individual woman remains: "Am I one of the ones who would get away without being raped, or one of the ones who wouldn't?"

In times of danger, it's almost impossible to think clearly. Fear sets off a rush of the chemical noradrenaline in the brain.

It cuts off access to higher-brain problem-solving skills. That's why it's important for every woman to have an escape plan and a self-defense plan ready and rehearsed before she goes out with a man. It's also important to memorize the danger signs of rape, look out for them, and be ready to get out at the earliest sign of threat. It takes skill to avoid danger and even greater skill to escape it. Every woman needs to learn those skills *before* danger comes.

> **No one has a right to come along later and say "You should have reacted differently." Any attempt to escape or survive is valid and honorable.**

Having strong skills in physical self-defense is important for every woman. So is learning to recognize rape warning signs in men and choosing to get away from men who show these signs. But none of those measures can guarantee safety. For any woman facing the threat of physical harm, it's a judgment call that she has to make alone. No one has a right to come along later and say, "You should have fought back," or "You should have just let him do it." *Any* attempt to escape or survive is valid and honorable.

Physical Force

Sex that's not consented to, but instead is done by force, is sometimes called "forcible rape." Legally, the forcible rape of a woman is the forced entry into her vagina, anus, or mouth. Usually the object used is a man's penis, although other objects are sometimes used, too.

Some Warning Signs of Rape

A man who has any of these characteristics might be a rapist:

- Emotionally abuses you (through insults, belittling comments, ignoring your opinion, or by acting sulky when you initiate an action or idea)
- Tells you who you may be friends with, how you should dress, or tries to control other elements of your life or relationship (he insists on picking the movie you'll see, the restaurant where you'll eat, and so on)
- Talks negatively about women in general
- Gets jealous when there's no reason
- Drinks heavily or uses drugs or tries to get you intoxicated
- Berates you for not wanting to get drunk, get high, have sex, or go with him to an isolated or personal place (his room, your apartment, or the like)
- Refuses to let you share any of the expenses of a date and gets angry when you offer to pay
- Is physically violent to you or others, even if it's "just" grabbing and pushing to get his way
- Acts in an intimidating way toward you (sits too close, uses his body to block your way, speaks as if he knows you much better than he does, touches you when you tell him not to)
- Is unable to handle sexual and emotional frustrations without becoming angry
- Doesn't view you as an equal, either because he's older or because he sees himself as smarter or socially superior
- Has a fascination with weapons
- Enjoys being cruel to animals, children, or people he can bully

Reprinted from *I Never Called It Rape* by Robin Warshaw. Used with permission.

For it to qualify legally as rape, the woman has to refuse sex, either by using words or by using her body to indicate refusal (shaking her head "no," for example). If she's too drunk or high to be able to refuse—for example, if she's passed out—then it's also considered rape. If she's under the legal age limit for her state, then it's called "statutory rape."

Men can be raped, too. The rapist is almost always another man. Usually men are raped anally, but some are raped orally. The rape of women is much more common, though, so that's the main focus of the following pages.

Why Don't Some Women Fight Back?

- They're afraid of being hurt or killed.
- What's happening makes no sense to them.
- Their brains are flooded with noradrenaline, so they can't think.
- Fighting back goes against their social training.
- They're in shock.
- The man might not seem like a rapist.
- They don't know they're being raped.
- They blame themselves.
- What's happening doesn't seem real.
- They feel crazy, and don't trust their perceptions and feelings.

A man's body weight and physical strength are the tools most often used in forcible rape. The man is able to hold the woman down, keep her from fighting back effectively, and force her into a position where he can put his penis inside her. Some men use ropes, neckties, belts, or electric cords to tie the woman down.

Some men work in pairs or groups, where one or more of them hold her down while each one "takes his turn." This is one form of "gang rape." There's been a lot of publicity lately about gang rapes at college fraternity parties. But those are nowhere near the only settings in which gang rapes have been known to happen.

Some rapists simply use enough force to complete the rape, but others also hit, cut, or otherwise injure their victims. Some women are killed before, during, or after the rape.

Let's say Don is a very troubled person. He never thought to question the cultural messages he heard about men and women when he was growing up. He believes that women are out to trick him and trap him, and that it's his job to prove his manhood. He believes that he can do this by making sexual conquests and by being physically strong and tough. He's mad at his mother, he's mad at his new female supervisor at work, and he's mad at every woman who ever turned him down for a date. He blames them for his feelings of powerlessness and worthlessness.

Don tried using seduction and psychological force on Sandy, but neither of those tactics worked. He's sexually aroused, and he's been taught to believe that he can't control his sexual urges. He's been drinking most of the evening, so his temper is up and his judgment is faulty. He's decided that Sandy is a tease, and that he's going to "take what's coming to him." He uses his arms and legs to pin her down while he opens her clothes and rapes her.

Why Don't Some Women Fight Back?

Let's say Sandy yells "no" and struggles against him. But she doesn't scream, and she can't get her arms free to hit him. Even if the woman doesn't struggle, it's still legally considered rape if she shakes her head or tells a man "no" and he penetrates her body anyway.

211

Some women don't fight back because they're afraid of being hurt or killed. In acquaintance rape—and particularly in date rape—many women don't fight back effectively because what's happening makes absolutely no sense to them. It goes against all their social training. Their brains may be experiencing noradrenaline flooding, so they can't think clearly. They're in shock, and they often don't realize they're being raped. Sometimes they don't understand what happened until many months—or many years—later.

In a date or acquaintance rape situation, the man may be someone the woman has known for a while. Often he's someone her friends admire. He doesn't fit the stereotype of the "mad rapist jumping out of the bushes." He's a "nice guy," and a nice guy wouldn't do something like that. She might blame herself. She's probably been well trained not to hit people or to "make a fuss." She might not scream because she's afraid of causing embarrassment—for herself or for the man. She might have been trained to believe that these kinds of reactions would make her less of a "lady."

On one hand, she knows that her body is being violated against her wishes. On the other hand, she has a lifetime of cultural training telling her that what's happening isn't really happening. She feels crazy.

Men Who Don't Know It's Rape

Women aren't the only ones who often deny the reality of rape. Many men who commit date rape also don't realize that that's what they're doing. In *I Never Called It Rape,* Robin Warshaw tells the story of a woman named Denise who was raped by a friend of a friend in her apartment. "He ignored her protests, pinned her to the bed with his body, and choked her. When he fell asleep after ejaculating, she escaped and drove to a friend's house."

When Denise and her friend returned the next morning, they found that the man had gone, but he'd left a note with a "smile face" drawn on it. It read, "Denise, I woke up and you were gone. Catch ya later! Have a nice day! Bob." Bob called minutes later, cheerful and friendly. She swore at him, told him never to call again, and hung up on him. "He called back, sounding surprised, asking, 'Hey, what's the matter?'"

A Man Who Doesn't Know It's Rape

- Might not know that "forced sex" is rape
- Might think it's part of a game, and his partner is in on the game
- Might think he's acting out a sexual fantasy
- Might stop if his partner tells him what he's doing is rape

---

When researchers interview men and women to find out if they've raped or been raped, the researchers usually don't use the word "rape." Instead they use a term like "forced sex." This is because many men *and women* are still in denial about the fact that it was rape—even years later, and even if their names aren't being recorded. If the researchers used the word "rape," they wouldn't get an accurate count.

In *I Never Called it Rape,* Warshaw reported on college students' answers to a *Ms.* magazine survey on date and acquaintance rape. In that survey, 84 percent of the men whose actions fit the legal definition of rape "said that what they did was *definitely* not rape."[2]

It's also helpful for women to know that men who rape aren't always aware that that's what's happening. In some cases women might stop the rape—or even prevent it—by naming it out loud, while it's happening. Ginny tells of the time she drove a man home from a party. It was someone she liked and respected, and he asked her up to his apartment for coffee. In his apartment he began kissing her and reaching inside her dress.

"I kept saying 'No! Cut it out!' and hitting at him, but he kept on pulling at my clothes. Pretty soon he was inside me—and then he had the incredible nerve to ask me how I felt. 'I feel like I'm being raped!' I said, loudly. He pulled out immediately and curled up at the foot of the sofa, with his head in his hands. He was apologizing all over the place. I got the impression he'd done this kind of thing before, but he'd never thought of it as rape. I got out of there."

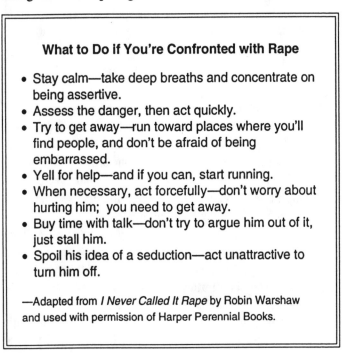

What to Do if You're Confronted with Rape

- Stay calm—take deep breaths and concentrate on being assertive.
- Assess the danger, then act quickly.
- Try to get away—run toward places where you'll find people, and don't be afraid of being embarrassed.
- Yell for help—and if you can, start running.
- When necessary, act forcefully—don't worry about hurting him; you need to get away.
- Buy time with talk—don't try to argue him out of it, just stall him.
- Spoil his idea of a seduction—act unattractive to turn him off.

—Adapted from *I Never Called It Rape* by Robin Warshaw and used with permission of Harper Perennial Books.

Many men who commit date rape might think their use of force is just part of a game. They might even tell themselves the woman is in on the game. They might think they're both acting out a sexual fantasy. But if a couple is really acting out a fantasy, both partners must freely agree beforehand on what can and can't take place. And if the fantasy includes any kind of force, then they agree beforehand on safeguards—including a "safe word" that either partner can use at any time to make the action stop immediately.

Sex that's forced against one partner's will isn't a fantasy. It's rape.

Breaking the Pattern

The fact that a man doesn't realize he's committing rape doesn't make him any less responsible for it. But learning about what does and doesn't qualify as rape can prompt a man to decide to get professional help. He can work on his attitudes and build his skills and options. He can learn to control his actions and find healthy outlets for anger. He can come to learn how much he's been controlled by destructive cultural messages. He can choose to replace those messages with healthy ones. He can speak out on the subject and help other men understand, too.[3]

Any woman can be raped, if she finds herself alone with a rapist and her skills in physical self-defense aren't strong enough. Any woman can be tricked into trusting a man who doesn't deserve her trust. No amount of emotional health, skill training, self-esteem, or awareness will give a woman 100-percent protection from sexual aggression. But there are many ways for a woman to lower her vulnerability to date rape.

The most important step toward self-protection is a woman's knowledge that she has a right to defend herself against sexual force. This is true even if she has to leave the situation just because she has a vague feeling that something's wrong. It's equally true if she has to "fight dirty" and really hurt the man who's trying to rape her—or yell, scream, and attract the attention of anyone who might be around. Warshaw also suggests that a woman try acting *very* unattractive, to spoil the attacker's illusion that she's really being seduced. Many women hesitate to take these kinds of extreme steps, for fear of being embarrassed. The question is this: Is it worse to be embarrassed or to be raped?

In almost all communities, and on most college campuses, training is available in physical self-defense. Tips in physical self-defense aren't included in this book because it's much harder to teach these skills without demonstration and practice. It's important that readers get hands-on training rather than just read a few tips and feel as if they know enough to stay safe. Some basic guidelines for finding training are included in the next chapter.

Systematic Desensitization—Playing the Continuum

Some highly skilled manipulators are well aware of all the points on the continuum of sexual aggression. They've learned how to "play" the continuum. This involves moving back and forth from less, to more, to less aggression. The aim is to make their partners feel crazy, so they'll doubt their perceptions and lower their defenses.

Although some women use this technique, too, it's more often used by men who plan to manipulate and/or rape women they're dating. A skillful sexual manipulator will often use this kind of process to slowly "desensitize" a woman to the fact that he's running over her boundaries. That's the focus of the following description.

216

He might begin early on the date, by making comments that are a little too sexual or aggressive. He might say things that are insulting toward women in general. She might be annoyed or suspicious, but tell herself the comments are harmless. Pretty soon he's being tender and sweet, and paying her compliments.

Signs of Systematic Desensitization

- Comments that are insulting or too sexual, too soon—followed by comments and gestures that are tender and sweet
- Getting more and more inappropriate, but each time backing off and being appropriate again
- Being threatening one moment and sensitive and seductive the next
- Being aggressive and dominant, then charming
- Making you doubt your perceptions and feelings
- Building you up and tearing you down, over and over, in little ways
- Putting your defenses to sleep
- Making it hard for you to keep track of your limits
- Making it seem like the confusion is your fault

The sexual comments become more and more inappropriate as the date wears on. Because she's let them slide so far, she feels as if it would be silly or wrong to object now. She's becoming less and less aware of her negative gut reactions. She's becoming used to them. He escalates into inappropriate touching—at first sensual, then sexual. They may still be in public at this point.

The woman is becoming desensitized to her own limits. The man pushes the process up, little by little, then backs off long enough to calm her fears. He might act slightly threatening one moment, and sensitive and seductive the next. She might feel as if something's wrong, but still question and doubt her own thoughts and feelings about the situation.

The Skill of the Manipulator

In this process the manipulator's skill is in knowing just how far he can invade a woman's boundaries without having her call the whole thing off. He pushes until she's almost angry enough—or scared enough—to take measures to stop him. Then he backs off and acts more appropriately until she's off her guard again. Each time, he's able to push a little farther.

There's a dynamic play between anger, fear, and shame. The manipulator redirects the partner's anger into fear, and fear into shame. He might turn from being aggressive to playing dumb—from anger and dominance to a little-boy charm. He gives mixed messages on purpose. When the woman gets confused, he subtly lets her know that *he's* okay—it's her confusion that's the problem.

This is a process in which the man alternately builds the woman up and tears her down. He does things that are psychologically painful, then he does other things that take the pain away. This is the kind of power that's used in brainwashing hostages and prisoners of war. It leaves her feeling powerless and defenseless—questioning her perceptions and even her sanity. This process is also common in ongoing abusive relationships. The message here is: "I have the power to hurt you or to make you feel good. It's your choice. Give me what I want and you'll get what you want." It's a false and twisted offer of empowerment.

If the woman has a history of being victimized—and particularly a history of abuse in childhood—she might be more likely to get taken in by this desensitization process. She might be so used to feeling powerless that she doesn't question it. She might have no concept of boundaries or limits, and no skills in setting or protecting them.

Getting Help

If you've ever used this kind of technique on others, you need professional help. Learning new attitudes and skills will be an important process, but you probably have other serious issues to work through, too. There are therapists who understand these issues and men's groups whose members have lived them.

If you've been the victim of this kind of process, you might also need professional help to explore your relationship with boundaries. But you can begin today to help protect yourself against being taken in again. The best protection includes:

1. Knowing how the desensitization process works—knowing how to recognize it and get out of the situation quickly.

2. Skills in setting boundaries and limits, enforcing them, and knowing when they're being violated.

3. Making sure you're with close and emotionally healthy friends on the first few dates, and asking them for honest feedback about your partner's behavior.

4. Realizing that you can't play this game and win. Any effort to reason with someone who's doing this will only feed the process. Just get out of the situation.

The systematic desensitization process is dangerous to those who don't understand it. But if a woman is alert and tuned in to her own gut feelings, it can be the early warning signal that saves her life. Once she realizes she might be in danger, she can decide what to do about it.

In this case the normal communication skills don't work. It won't help her at all to set better limits with him, because he'll just jump over them. And telling him how she feels about what he's doing will only fan the flames. The best thing to do is to get out.

Why Do Some Men Become Aggressive?

Men who are skilled in understanding women are much less likely to be forceful or manipulative. They know how to meet women's needs—and how to attract women who are likely to meet their needs. They know how to invite women into relationships and how to work toward setting mutual goals and limits. They see the full range of choices. They consider themselves worthy, capable, and deserving of respect. For that reason, they're free to see women as worthy, capable, and deserving of respect.

Men's motives in using sexual force or manipulation can be as complicated as the men themselves. These motives might have to do with fear, frustration, anger, dependence, cultural standards, lack of confidence, feelings of powerlessness, fear of losing control, or a learned tendency to see women as objects. A man who rapes might even believe he's in love with his victim. But all these motives follow a single pattern: Men use sexual aggression because, at that moment, they believe it's the best way—or the only way—to get what they think they need.

What a sexually aggressive man thinks he needs can be any of a number of things. It might just be sex. The man might have a low enough opinion of himself to believe that no woman would choose to have sex with him, so he feels he has to "take it" or trick her into it. Or he might feel a need to conform to the cultural standard that says men are supposed to be in control at all times—and that they're supposed to be aggressive and dominate women. He might be afraid that a failure to meet that standard would make him less of a man.

Why Do Some Men Become Sexually Aggressive?

They believe, at that moment, it's the best way—or the only way—to get what they need. What do they think they need?

- Sex—they might not believe anyone would really want them.
- Proof of their manhood—living up to the cultural standard.
- Power—they might believe that real power is power over others.
- Revenge—women might have hurt them long ago.

A sexually aggressive man might believe that he needs power and that making another person physically or emotionally helpless is the best or only way to get it. A man might believe he needs revenge against a woman—or "type" of woman—who used or abused him years ago. Making a woman feel degraded or humiliated might appear to bring temporary relief from his pain. The woman he's raping might be a symbol to him, instead of a real person whose feelings matter.

In any case there's a need—real or imagined. There are strong fears behind that need, strong enough to push him toward the use of force. Please remember this, though: It's not a rational need. Usually it's primitive, driven by emotions from the deeper regions of the brain.

If a woman tries to use logic to talk a man out of rape, it usually doesn't work. His actions aren't being controlled by his higher brain. And if he's under the influence of alcohol or other drugs, he can also be very unpredictable. The situation can easily turn more violent. Under that influence, he might go through a psychological process that's very much like the personality "switching" that takes place in people with multiple personality disorder. If one of a man's "personalities" is violent, the woman may not know it until it's too late.

> **If a woman tries to use logic to talk a man out of rape, it usually doesn't work. His actions aren't being controlled by his higher brain.**

Help for Sexually Aggressive Men

If you're a man who has used sexual force or manipulation, it's important to question yourself carefully. What kinds of fears might be hiding underneath your aggressive actions? What needs do you believe those actions will help you meet? There are always other ways of making sure your true needs are met. If you need new skills, there are many good places to get skill training. If you need to resolve the effects of childhood trauma, you can get help from professionals.

Counseling should be a first priority. All men who have raped—and many who have used seduction and psychological force—need counseling, *immediately*. There will always be some men who don't respond to treatment. Their urge to rape or manipulate might come from a mental illness that's so severe it doesn't allow them to care about the damage they're doing. But for most men, there's hope. You can learn to identify your true needs and find better ways of meeting them. If your aggression is the result of a brain chemical imbalance, psychiatrists can prescribe medication to bring you back into balance.

Men are often trained to believe that "real men" don't need to get help. They're taught that they have to do it all alone—

that it's not okay to talk about their feelings and experiences. But all men—and particularly men who are locked into aggressive patterns—need to talk to other men. You can find support in groups of men who are going through the same thing. You can learn skills to help you deal with the pain behind your aggression.[4]

You can also get in the habit of talking to women as friends and really listening to what they have to say. Find out who they are, how they feel, and how sexual aggression affects them. Read things women have written about the effects of rape. Learn to care about women as human beings.

Men are taught that they shouldn't need help, or need to talk. But all men—and particularly men with aggressive patterns—need to talk to other men.

Women Who Want to Help

Women can also help men in general learn to understand and care about women. A woman can send clear, consistent messages that let all the men she meets know that women are worthy of respect and friendship.

But remember: **If a man has been sexually violent with you, it's not your job to "fix" him.** You're the last person who would ever be able to help him. If you feel a need to fix his problems, then you're also suffering from a problem, and you'll need therapy to help you overcome it. Your job is to protect yourself.

Any feeling that calls you to put yourself in the way of a sexual threat isn't love. It's a feeling that the man—or society as a whole—has programmed into you. It has everything to do with control, and nothing to do with love. If you try to be his therapist and help him change, it will only help him become more violent in the future. It will also put you at greater and greater risk.

If a man you know needs help for sexual violence, tell him he needs therapy. Give him the number of a good therapist or self-help group, if you have one. Then get out. End the relationship. If he's willing to get help, he'll get it. If he's not, you can't help him. But you can at least save yourself. You can't help anyone by being a victim.

Notes

1. All of these examples are common techniques that sexually aggressive men have used to get women to comply. For more information see the rape literature cited in the Bibliography, including Robin Warshaw's *I Never Called It Rape* and many of the articles in Parrot and Bechhofer's *Acquaintance Rape: The Hidden Crime.*
2. For more information, see Robin Warshaw's I Never Called It Rape.
3. The Bibliography lists several books for men, about men and violence, and about being a man in general. These include Timothy Beneke's Men on Rape, Allan Creighton and Paul Kivel's *Helping Teens Stop Violence,* Paul Kivel's *Men's Work,* John Lee's *The Flying Boy* and *Facing the Fire* (with Bill Scott), and John Stoltenberg's *The End of Manhood.* The Bibliography also lists several books that address anger in general.
4. Men's groups now exist in many communities. They deal with issues of violence, plus the full range of issues men face. Many community mental health centers offer individual and group therapy for men who have histories of violence. If you're starting your own group, the *Worth Protecting* workbook offers exercises. So do the *Men's Work* workbooks by Paul Kivel, and *Helping Teens Stop Violence* by Creighton and Kivel.

Journal Questions

1. Describe a situation where it might be difficult to tell the difference between seduction and psychological force.

2. "Systematic desensitization" is a process that takes place in many areas of life and throughout people's lives. It's often called "getting used to things." What are some healthy and unhealthy desensitization processes you've experienced in your life?

3. When you read the sections on seduction, psychological force, threat of physical force, and physical force, what emotional reactions (if any) did you have? What did these reactions tell you about yourself and your experiences?

CHAPTER 11

The Effects of Sexual Aggression

Every act of aggression has many victims. For example, look at the rape of a woman by a man she's been dating. The woman suffers—sometimes for years—with effects that run from troubling to tragic. The man also suffers, slipping deeper into the fears and frustrations that drove his actions. The society that bred the rape suffers, too, because most of our actions have "ripple" effects far beyond the effects we can see. The world becomes just a little less safe, a little less respectful, and a little less kind.

> **The "game" of sexual aggression has no winners. This chapter looks at the effects of sexual aggression on its victims and on the people who use it.**

There are two kinds of people who need this chapter: men and women. If you're a man with a history of sexual aggression, you need to understand the pain that women go through during and after rape or sexual manipulation. You may have been trained to tell yourself that manipulation is "just part of the game" and that rape is "just playing a little rough." If so, then understanding the effects will help you understand that these aren't games and women aren't toys.

You also need to understand the harmful effects that sexual force and manipulation can have on the people who use them. People who really have their own best interests in mind don't rape people or trick them into having sex. They respect themselves and the other person too much.

If you've been raped, it's important to know that all your feelings about it are valid and normal. They shouldn't be covered up, denied, rushed, or reasoned away. There are some predictable patterns that many people go through after being raped. It helps to recognize those patterns, to know that you're not crazy or "wrong" to be feeling that way.

But if you've been raped and your reactions don't follow those patterns, that doesn't mean it wasn't really rape. Many women have been trained all their lives to deny their anger. Also, many people who were abused as children often feel as if their bodies aren't really part of them. They might take sexual abuse for granted. That's a way of protecting themselves from their real feelings. If you were forced or frightened into having sex, then you were raped—no matter what feelings you do or don't have, during or after the rape.

If you were forced or frightened into having sex, then you were raped—no matter what feelings you do or don't have, during or after the rape.

If you're a woman and you've never been raped or sexually manipulated, congratulations! Knowing about the effects will help you understand why it's so important to make sure your vulnerability to these things is as low as possible.

This chapter looks first at the effects of four kinds of sexual aggression—seduction, psychological force, threat of physical force, and physical force—on the people who are manipulated or forced into having sex. Then it explores the effects of sexual aggression on the people who use it. To simplify the text, some of these sections are worded as if all the victims of aggression are women, even though that's not always the case in real life.

Effects on the Victims

Seduction

People usually don't think of seduction as having any negative effects at all. If the person who's been seduced is emotionally vulnerable, though, the effects can be serious. If seduction is a "leading away" from the realities of life, then pretty soon we have to return to reality. If reality was messy before, it'll still be messy after seduction. It might even have become messier.

In a way, it's like getting drunk or high for an evening. The escape feels good, but the next day's hangover, headaches, jitters, shakes, and other effects feel rotten. Often people find that they forgot to do something they really needed to do, or did something they'll have to dig themselves out of now. People can keep paying for years for something they did in two seconds when they were drunk or high.

If reality was messy before, it'll still be messy after seduction. It might even have become messier. And the chance for friendship has been damaged.

One of the main problems with seduction is that our culture has taught many people to mistake it for a sign of genuine caring and commitment. It has some of the same characteristics—physical closeness, caresses, soft words—but physical intimacy isn't the same as emotional intimacy. Sometimes becoming physically close can push people farther apart. This is especially true if it happens too soon—before both partners are emotionally ready—or if one or the other partner is using the other to "get" something, like sex or emotional security.

Many people have let themselves be seduced, telling themselves it will lead to love. Most wake up just as lonely as they were before, but with more bitterness and less self-confidence. Many couples have failed to find friendship because they pushed into physical intimacy before they'd had a chance to become friends.

Psychological Force

Psychological force—"hard-core manipulation"—is a kind of emotional violence. If you've ever been pushed into doing anything by someone who used guilt, fear of loss, or social threat, then you know how insulting and "crazy-making" manipulation can be. It may have been your choice to give in to the manipulation, but you still know in your gut that the tactics the other person used weren't fair. Your choice wasn't made freely.

When the result of the manipulation is sex, the negative feelings are much more intense. It's a violation of boundaries, both psychological and physical. What you've given up is something precious—your choice in one of the most private and personal areas of your life. And you've been tricked into giving up that choice. You've been betrayed. When betrayal leads to an act as personal and physically intimate as sex, the emotional price can be high.

The fact that you consented to the sex doesn't make it any less a betrayal. It just adds a layer of self-betrayal. Many

230

people wonder how they could have fallen for "the oldest lines in the book." Well, there's a reason those lines are so old and so well used. Spoken with the right amount of skill, they can be very effective. And the full force of your social training can be pointing you toward believing them—at least for a while. Here's where the old denial skills take over.

> In manipulation, the fact that you consented to the sex doesn't make it any less a betrayal. It just adds a layer of self-betrayal.

Sexual manipulation isn't as dramatic as rape, but its effects can be serious. It can lead people—particularly women—to feel helpless, hopeless, bitter, depressed, angry, and worthless. Some women blame themselves for being "taken in," so they stop trusting their intuition and their judgment. But the truth is that it wasn't their intuition or their true judgment that led them to give in to the psychological force. If they'd been listening to those things, they would never have been fooled.

Threat of Physical Force

This crime is on the border between manipulation and force. It combines the effects of the two. Here the tool used in manipulation is the fear of being trapped, physically hurt, injured, or killed. Coerced rape can cause the same kinds of intense fear, anger, self-blame, and self-hatred that forcible rape can cause.

For the woman who's had sex under the threat of force, the fear can continue long after the rape. The memory of the terror of physical harm can be very real. She was under someone else's control, and she believed that he had the power to kill her. She has the added burden of knowing that she *chose* to believe the threat, and the self-blame and self-doubt can make life miserable: "Maybe I should have fought back. Maybe he really wouldn't have hurt me. How could I be so gullible?"

> **A woman scared into sex was under the man's control and thought he had the power to kill her. But later her self-doubt can still make life miserable.**

Often well-meaning family, friends, police, and others will make things worse by telling her what they think she could or should have done differently. They usually don't realize that these kinds of comments make the self-blame and self-doubt much worse. The truth is that, in coerced rape, it simply isn't possible to be sure whether or not the man is going to carry out his threats. Faced with these threats, a woman takes her best guess at how to survive.

Afterward, all she or anyone else needs to know is that she wasn't responsible for what happened; she dealt with the situation as well as she could, and she survived it. She can plan for the future and learn better self-protection skills. But worrying about what she might have done differently is useless and self-destructive.

Physical Force

Many people believe the effects of rape by an acquaintance would be less painful than the effects of rape by a stranger. But in fact, many women suffer more serious effects. Because it was committed by someone they knew, many women feel a stronger sense of having been betrayed. They trusted the man, so they often have stronger feelings of guilt and self-betrayal. They may lose the ability to trust their own intuition and sense of trust. Acquaintance rape can turn a woman's thoughts and feelings about herself, friendship, dating, and relationships upside-down.

As the earlier chapters have shown, the fact that the woman knows the man can make it harder for her to protect herself. Unfortunately, though, it doesn't keep her from feeling all the pain, fear, anxiety, depression, humiliation, anger, guilt, shame, and self-hatred that often follow rape. Rape is a form of physical, emotional, and spiritual violence. Violence at the hand of someone you know and trust can hurt much more than violence from a stranger.

After rape—even by someone you know—the pain, fear, anxiety, depression, humiliation, anger, guilt, shame, and self-hatred can last many, many years.

For many women it's not just that they feel bad as a result of the rape. It's also that their lives are thrown off balance, sometimes for a long time. The fear can be so intense that it becomes hard to hold down a job, have a social life, and do all the things people need to do to live healthy, responsible lives. The effects of rape can ruin jobs, friendships, and marriages.

After rape a woman's feelings of anger, bitterness, and humiliation can be so deep that it becomes impossible to have sex—even with people she really cares about and who really care about her. The partners of people who've been raped sometimes have problems of their own adjusting to the rape. Men whose wives or girlfriends have been raped sometimes feel as if their own manhood has been threatened by the rape. And even though they don't mean any harm, their reaction

233

can make things much worse for the woman who's been raped.

Women who have been forced to have sex tend to ask themselves the same questions as those who have been raped at the threat of force: What did I do wrong? What could I have done differently? The truth is, no matter what she did or might have done differently, she's still not responsible for the fact that it happened. Unfortunately, though, even the best intentions can't keep friends and would-be helpers from saying things that make her feel more and more guilty and ashamed.

If the woman decides to press charges, the fact that the rapist was an acquaintance can also set her up for more trouble. The law itself treats rape as rape no matter who commits it. But some people in the criminal justice process might still buy into old mistaken beliefs about women and sexual aggression. Friends and family members might share those beliefs. Their reactions—even subtle ones—can increase the woman's feelings of self-blame.

For many people who have been raped, that mistaken sense of self-blame is the most destructive effect. Some people blame themselves simply because they've been trained to blame themselves. Others do it because other people appear to be blaming them. Many people who've been victimized tend to blame themselves for the same reasons they blamed themselves for what happened to them as children: because it makes them feel safer. They're afraid to admit that something happened that was completely out of their control. They also find it scary to admit that bad things sometimes happen to good people—that life isn't fair. If they can tell themselves it was their fault, they feel a false sense of control and justice.

Rape—by force or by the threat of force—is traumatic. Many people who have been raped continue to suffer from post-traumatic stress disorder, the illness first described in chapter seven. Again, the symptoms of PTSD can include intense fear, difficulty sleeping, anger or rage, guilt, numbness, depression, nightmares and flashbacks (strong memories of the event), problems with concentration or memory, and substance abuse or other addictive behaviors.

> **If you've been raped, remember: It wasn't your fault—no matter how you feel now, no matter who did it, and no matter what you did or didn't do.**

How intense the effects of sexual aggression may be—and how long they last—is different for different people. Some say they feel "recovered" after a few weeks, while others are just starting to feel emotionally healthy again after ten years. Some feel the effects in most aspects of their lives, and others work through the trauma and move on quickly. Some feel only mild symptoms and mistake that as a sign that they weren't really raped. Too many people deny or "stuff" their anger, denying they need or deserve help.

Many people who have been raped go through a grieving process, a lot like the process people go through when someone dies or when a job or relationship ends. Grieving isn't a bad thing. It's a necessary part of life. Grieving, and the healing process in general, are given more attention in the next chapter. But first, one important reminder:

Whether or not you've been raped isn't measured by how many bruises you have, how bad you feel afterward, or how long it takes you to recover. If you've been forced to have sex, you've been raped. If you've had sex because you feared physical force or harm, you've been raped. What happened to you was wrong. It wasn't your fault—no matter how you feel now, no matter who did it, and no matter what you did or didn't do.

Effects on People Who Use Sexual Force

In our society we're trained to separate "victims" and "victimizers" into neat little piles. We think the victim of force is the only one who suffers, and the person who uses force somehow "wins." We have this image of a grinning villain "getting away" with something. But the truth isn't anywhere near that simple.

Most people who use or abuse others do it because they believe that's the way the world works. Usually they learned it as children—by being used or abused themselves, or by watching someone they loved hurt someone else they loved. That buried an intense fear deep inside them. As children, they couldn't protect themselves or their loved ones. As adults, they try to protect themselves by being forceful, but they can never relax their guard. Every time they see the limits of their power, they're terrified. There's no such thing as enough power.

Aggressive and manipulative acts come from feelings of pain, powerlessness, fear, and anger. Hurting or using others may feel like the only way to be safe or to get what we need. It doesn't work, though: Every time we use force against someone else, we end up feeling less safe and more defensive. That leads to more aggressive acts. That's why the tendency to use sexual force is sometimes described as "progressive." It gets worse, because "scratching the itch" just makes it "itch" worse.

Seduction

The effects of using seduction might be mild compared to the effects of raping someone. They can still be serious, though. Many people have seduced others, only to find the others hopelessly "in love" and pursuing them. Some people who feel they've been used sexually have been known to do

236

some pretty drastic things in return: call the seducer over and over again, show up at his or her job, park outside his or her home, introduce themselves to his or her spouse, etc. Most people don't react this way to being seduced, but it takes only one to cause quite a few problems.

And then, of course, there's always the risk of pregnancy or sexually transmitted disease. If this person is letting you seduce him or her, isn't it possible that others have also succeeded? Isn't there a chance that one of them might have been HIV positive?

The seducer can find him- or herself in a messy situation, pick up a life-threatening disease, and lose the ability to trust his or her emotions.

Another problem with seduction is that the person who's being seduced isn't the only one who can get seduction confused with love. For the one being seduced, the danger is that seduction will look like love. But for the seducer, the danger is that everything—including real love—will start to look like seduction. Seducers lose their ability to trust their emotions.

Seducers also get addicted to the adrenalin rush of the chase. As soon as the person is "caught" and it's no longer a game, they feel "let down." Many people who are caught up in seduction games let person after person slip out of their lives. Some of these people might have made excellent long-term partners.

Psychological Force

Psychological force has special dangers for the person who uses it. It's hard to go around fooling other people without, sooner or later, getting in the habit of fooling yourself. Lying to others often gets in the way of your ability to see the truth. People who can't be trusted also seem to have a hard time trusting the ones who truly deserve their trust. They might keep all their defenses up against people who treat them well—only to get taken in by others who are just as manipulative as they are.

Manipulation—whether it's seduction or psychological force—is inspired by fear. It's a response to the fear that we can't get what we want or need any other way. There may be anger mixed in with that fear. Fear feels bad, and anger is a common way of trying to defend ourselves.

People who use psychological force can lose their ability to see the truth, to trust people who deserve their trust, and to resist other "con artists."

When we act out of fear, it sends a message to our subconscious minds. That message says that the fear is real, the fear is important, and we have no defense against it. Acting out of fear makes it grow bigger and more powerful. The more we use manipulation to get what we want, the less we can believe in our ability to get it any other way.

Threat of Physical Force

Using the threat of physical force on another can have all the effects of using psychological force but at much higher levels. This can be true even if the person who used it tells himself that he was never really going to use physical force. Underneath it all, he'll know that the other person was scared and acted only out of fear. The whole event was based on fear.

Using the threat of force to rape someone also has many of the effects of using physical force. It can bring prosecution and imprisonment. Many men who use these tactics don't really think it's rape, especially if they don't plan to carry out their threats. But in the eyes of the law, the threat of force is all that's needed to make it rape. For example, if the man says he has a gun in the glove compartment, he doesn't even have to show the gun. He can still be convicted.

Physical Force

Forcible rape also carries the possibility of prosecution and imprisonment, whether or not the force was enough to leave bruises and other marks. And like the use of psychological or physical threats, it throws the person who uses it further and further back into fear. It confirms his belief that the world is ruled by force and run by attack. In a world like that, no one would be safe. It's no wonder people who rape become more and more fearful as time passes.

> **People who rape become more and more fearful, and feel less and less good about themselves. They also risk being arrested and going to prison.**

Like any act of violence, physical force also damages the person who uses it. There are many explanations. Some people believe in a universal law that says "You reap what you sow," or, "What goes around comes around." Others believe that people eventually bring punishment on themselves because they feel guilty about things they've done. Some believe that all people are spiritually connected, so whatever we do to others, we're also doing to ourselves. Whatever explanation you choose, you may have noticed that hurting others makes it harder to feel good about yourself—even if you believed your actions were justified.

Of course, even if sexual aggression didn't hurt the people who used it, it still wouldn't be right. But knowing that something is wrong isn't always enough to keep us from doing it. We need to know all the possible effects of our actions—on others and on ourselves. We also need to know what our other choices are.

This book has tried to balance information about sexual force with advice on how to live happily without it. Part VI, and the *Worth Protecting* workbook, give more suggestions for building a lifestyle free of force and manipulation. If you ever have doubts about whether you want to try out those suggestions, please remember this chapter. Remember how you've been hurt and/or hurt others. Please know you have the choice to end those patterns now.

Journal Questions

1. If you've been forced or manipulated into having sex, how would you describe your reactions afterward? How did or do those reactions look like the reactions described in this chapter? How were they different?

2. If you've used sexual force or manipulation on someone else, what do you think of the way this chapter described the effects of using force or manipulation? Do you think any of those effects might be true in your case?

3. If you've used force or manipulation, what's your reaction to reading about the effects of that on another person? If you've been the victim of those things, what's your reaction to reading about how they've affected the people who used them?

PART VI

Hope and
Healing

CHAPTER 12

The Healing Process

This chapter is an introduction to the healing process. What's needed might be healing from sexual force or manipulation, or it might be healing from a history that makes force or manipulation feel like the only choice. The chapter is written for people who use sexual aggression and for people who suffer at its hands. We all need healing.

Obviously, this chapter won't heal anyone by itself. Healing is a long process that no book—and certainly no chapter—can do for you. But it's important to take a look at some of the work that needs to be done and some of the help that's available. And it's most important to know that there's hope.

In any healing process, the first step is to take an honest look at the problem. If you break a bone, you need an X ray. If you've been raped, you need to admit that it's happened and it's going to need healing. If you have signs of PTSD, you need to know that they won't go away by themselves.

If you've been using sexual aggression, you need to call it what it is and admit that it's a problem—*your problem*. If you're abusing others or being abused—and it might be linked to other troubles in your past or present life—you need to make a commitment to get help and healing for those troubles. You need to take responsibility for your own healing process.

This chapter looks at the need to

- let others into the healing process;
- build skills to reduce fear and danger;
- know and accept the feelings of grieving; and
- let go of broken dreams and rebuild hope.

The next step is to find and accept help from other people. Usually that means trying to keep your mind as open as possible. You've begun a process of understanding and grieving over what's happened to you, learning to do things differently, and rebuilding hope and meaning in your life.

Letting Others In

It sounds so simple to say it: If we need healing, we also need help from other people. But nothing can be more important—or more difficult to admit. Our culture teaches us—particularly men—that strong, brave people are the ones who do it all themselves, never show their feelings, never ask for help, and never accept help. That's complete nonsense. Most of those people aren't strong or brave. They're just closed-minded and emotionally constipated. They miss out on good ideas, important human experiences, and a chance to grow and understand. They're very, very frightened, and they let their fear cage them in.

The strong, brave people are the ones who accept help and caring from others. It can be terrifying at first, because most of us were taught from our earliest days to be deeply ashamed of the fact that we aren't perfect. But only by letting healthy people into our lives can we really understand that our flaws don't make us any less lovable or any less worthy. When we let others help us grow stronger, we realize that they're also growing stronger as a result. And when we reach out to help someone else, we find that it helps us, too.

> **The help and healing process takes time and energy. But pushing the feelings "underground" and being self-destructive take more time and energy.**

For healing from PTSD and the other effects of rape or childhood abuse, you'll need both professional help and the help of others who have gone through—or are going through—the same healing process. You might need to learn self-defense techniques, so you can lower the level of fear and avoid being revictimized. If you need to work on your communication and assertiveness skills, you'll learn more if you let others into your learning process. If you've victimized someone else, you'll also need professional help and the help of others who are trying to learn to live without the use of force.

If dependence on alcohol or other drugs has made you more likely to abuse others or be abused, you may need treatment, and you'll certainly need an ongoing program of recovery. Many people find that it helps to work with a therapist and also get involved in a mutual support group of people with the same problem. This can be a powerful combination for healing.

Please remember this: Many people have had experiences that have wounded them—physically, sexually, emotionally, or spiritually. It takes time and energy to get help and go through the healing process. But it takes much more time and energy to keep pushing the uncomfortable feelings down, and to keep getting caught up in destructive or self-destructive life patterns.

Skills That Reduce Fear and Danger

Whenever we're injured, it's important to go through a careful healing process. But the first thing to do is to lower our level of immediate danger. We need to put out the fire—or get out of the house—before we start treating our burns.

It's the same way with the effects of trauma, abuse, and sexual aggression. If we're feeling blocked and paralyzed by fear, we won't be able to give the healing process the attention it needs. If we're in danger of being revictimized, then we're in danger of having our wounds made deeper and harder to heal.

To reduce fear and danger, we need skills in:
- self-knowledge
- self-respect and respect of others
- recognizing boundaries and setting limits
- friendship
- clear and direct communication and assertiveness
- recognizing choice points
- sorting out responsibilities
- making decisions
- recognizing danger
- accepting help
- building relationships in slow, careful ways
- physical self-defense

The skills described in this book, and in the *Worth Protecting* workbook, are important ones for self-protection. These include skills in self-knowledge, self-respect, respect for others, recognizing boundaries, setting limits, friendship, clear and direct communication, assertiveness, recognizing choice points, sorting out responsibilities, making decisions, recognizing danger, accepting help, and building relationships in slow and careful ways. There are also many other books, courses, and groups that can help you learn and practice these and other important skills.

If the experience of trauma has left you with emotionally paralyzing fear, you'll need a course of therapy that deals with both the trauma and the fear. As part of the healing process, you can work at understanding the kinds of memories, beliefs, and thoughts that lead to the fear. But it's important not to let anyone take away your defenses—including denial and lack of trust—before you have the strength to operate safely without them.

Most professionals can be trusted, but so can the wisdom of your own body and emotions. It's always frightening to go through a healing process. But if you don't feel safe in your relationship with your therapist or counselor, take steps to get safe. That might mean talking to others who have been through experiences like yours. It might mean checking out the credentials of your therapist. Or it might mean switching to a therapist whose personal style feels less threatening to you. Your own safety—emotional and spiritual as well as physical—is worth protecting.

If you've been sexually assaulted, it will also be important to lower your vulnerability to attack in the future. You don't need to become a martial arts expert, though—unless that's always been a dream of yours. Through your local YWCA or rape counseling center, you can find out about self-defense courses that are tailored to the needs of women who want to raise their level of safety. If you're a woman recovering from rape, you might be better off in a group of all women. You're probably feeling emotionally vulnerable to begin with. It might be best to talk about these things among people who have had the same experience.

When you look into self-defense courses, watch out for a few things. Avoid organizations or courses that do what's sometimes called "rape reenactment" or "rape-proofing." In these courses people are put through experiences that raise some of the same feelings as being attacked by a real rapist. The idea is to teach self-defense in a realistic setting. But these exercises can put women into intense feelings of fear and powerlessness, and even trigger symptoms of PTSD. They can be dangerous to the woman and to the healing process. And beware of any course that makes big promises. It's much better to go with something low-key and practical.

Besides the physical ways of getting away from an attacker, your training should also include ways of spotting danger in people you think are your friends, and getting out of the situation before the attack starts. Rape by dates or acquaintances can be very different from rape by strangers. It's not just a matter of self-defense. It's also a matter of social awareness, skills, and flexibility.

The Feelings of Grief

Sometimes it helps to think about the healing process in the words that people have used to describe grieving. Grieving isn't just something we do when someone dies. Whenever something happens that causes intense pain or trauma, there's usually some kind of loss. We might lose our feelings of safety or our dream of a perfect life or relationship. We might lose our illusion that we're all powerful and in control. In any case, something we value has been lost. Grieving will be an important part of the healing process.

Some Common Feelings of Grief
- Denial
- Self-Blame
- Depression
- Isolation
- Anger
- Acceptance

Grieving is more than just being sad or crying. It includes a lot of different thoughts and feelings. The grieving process has often been described as taking place in stages, but it's more useful to think of these as feeling states that come and go. The feelings of grieving aren't very predictable, and different people call them by different names. But whatever names you use, knowing about the feelings can help you remember that what you're going through is normal.

Here are a few of the emotions of grieving that people have identified:

• *Denial*: When we tell ourselves it didn't really happen, or it wasn't really all that bad.

• *Self-Blame*: When we feel guilty and concentrate on what we could have done differently.

• *Depression*: When we feel hopeless—like nothing we can do will make any difference—and we find it hard to do anything.

• *Isolation*: When we avoid being open and intimate with other people, and even feel alone when we're with people.

• *Anger*: When our feelings of anger over what happened become very powerful and sometimes invade other areas of our lives.

• *Acceptance*: When we make peace with the fact that we suffered loss, grow stronger from the experience, and go on to live full lives.

Here's a discussion of how each of these feelings helps us heal, and what happens when we get "stuck" in that feeling.

Denial

Denial is a funny thing. It can be our best friend or a stubborn enemy. When the truth is too painful to deal with, denial is an important—and sometimes life-saving—skill. For example, what happens to children who live in families where there's substance abuse or addiction, or physical, sexual, or emotional abuse? They can't be honest with themselves about what the people they love and depend on are doing. It would be too terrible. And if they were honest with others about what's going on, the effects would probably get even worse.

If as an adult you've been attacked by someone you knew and trusted, you also need to protect yourself. For a while you might need to tell yourself that what happened wasn't really an attack, or tell yourself it wasn't serious. This gives you time to build up more strength so you can be prepared when it's time to accept the truth. Only you will know when that time comes.

If we never let go of denial, though, we never come to grips with what happened to us. We never admit that what happened really mattered—and that *we* really matter. We never get the help we need to start the healing process. Denial shouldn't be "broken down" or "crashed through." But people who are in denial need to build up strength and safety. Only when we feel safe can we let go of the denial and begin to deal with the truth.

Self-Blame

At first, self-blame is another important "survival skill." Again, take the example of a child living in a painful situation. The child might blame him- or herself for what's happening in the family. Then the child doesn't have to deal with the fact that it's all completely beyond his or her control. That fact would be terrifying to a small child who really has no other choices.

Even as adults we sometimes blame ourselves for what's happened to us. For one thing, the people around us may be acting as if it was our fault. It's also frightening to admit that bad things can happen to good people and that things happen that don't make any sense. There's so much in life that's beyond our control. Sometimes it feels safer just to take the blame. That way we can pretend we're in control, that things make sense, and that justice wins out.

> **Self-blame helps us feel more in control, but it often becomes more painful than the fears it's trying to hide. We lose sight of all our choices and our freedom.**

The trouble is that those things aren't true. We're often not in control, events don't always make sense, and unfair things do happen. We can't cover that up forever. There will always be more things that don't seem fair and don't make sense. We can't take the blame for all of it.

What's worse, self-blame often becomes more painful than the fears it was meant to cover. It teaches us to hate ourselves. We start to attract more pain, almost as if we were punishing ourselves. When we're caught up in self-blame, we never learn the truth about what happened to us in the past, and we lose sight of all the choices we have in the present. Of course we need to take responsibility for our actions. But that's very different from blaming ourselves for things that were beyond our control.

Life gets better if we can heal the self-blame. We need to accept that there are many things beyond our control, and that things happen that aren't logical or fair. That hurts, but we do have choices, and we have many sources of help and strength. Whatever challenges come up, we'll be able to face them.[1]

Depression

When people are physically paralyzed, they can't move. Depression can be described as an emotional paralysis that affects every area of life. Depression can have many symptoms, including crying a lot, feeling emotionally numb, feeling empty and scared, feeling hopeless, feeling incompetent, feeling powerless, having no appetite, eating compulsively, abusing alcohol or other drugs, feeling unable to move, or feeling like anything you do will be useless. Depression is a lot more—and a lot more serious—than just being lazy or feeling sorry for ourselves. It's as if the whole world has become strange and we're not completely alive.

As a normal part of the grieving process, depression lets us pull back from life for a while and "lick our wounds." At times when we're grieving, we need all the energy we have just for the grieving itself. Depression is a way of keeping ourselves from using that energy on normal life functions. But if we get stuck in depression, it can get in the way of our other needs and purposes in life. It can take away our ability to support ourselves and be healthy in relationships. It can rob us of the energy we need to do the other work of healing. And it can lead to thoughts of suicide.

> **Depression lets us pull back and "lick our wounds." But if we get stuck in it, it keeps us from living fully and fulfilling our purposes. It can also be dangerous.**

Some grief counselors say that if depression goes on for more than six months, it might be more than a normal part of grieving. It might be what they call "clinical depression." Professional help might be needed.

Depression can be caused by a number of things, including diet problems, substance abuse, anger that hasn't been dealt with, isolation, or chemicals in the body or brain that are out of balance. It's important to get help in finding out what the cause of the depression is. If there's a physical cause, there's a physical solution. If the causes are emotional, we can get help in working these out, too.

Whatever the cause of the depression might be, it's important to get out in the world, do things, and be with emotionally healthy people—even though the depression tells us that those are the *last* things we'd want to do.[2]

Isolation

One of the most dangerous things that people in any grieving or healing process can do is to isolate. In isolation, we close ourselves off from ideas, help, affection, and questions—and from sources of spiritual strength. We can think crazy thoughts and make them sound like they make sense. We can start to believe we're worthless or unlovable. Anger, fear, and pain can grow larger than life. Isolation can be both a cause and an effect of depression or substance abuse. We sometimes isolate by being alone, but that's not the only way to do it. We can be isolated in a room full of people.

Isolation isn't the same as solitude. In solitude we feel a sense of wholeness and connectedness, even though we're alone. Solitude feels like a choice, made from a position of strength. In isolation we feel incomplete and trapped.

Like any other kind of seduction, isolation leads us away from our own lives. It robs us of mental, emotional, social, and spiritual nourishment.

If we've been hurt by other people, isolation can be very tempting. We might feel as if other people are the problem, and isolation is the solution. But like any other kind of seduction, isolation leads us away from our own lives. It robs us of mental, emotional, social, and spiritual nourishment. It takes away our options. Like most self-destructive acts, isolation might seem dramatic—even romantic—at first. But it soon gets boring and predictable. The healing process needs other people because we all need other people.

Anger

At first anger is meant to protect us. It's the response of our body and brain to a threat. It's the decision to fight back, to defend our dignity. It's the understanding that "No! I didn't deserve this, and I won't let it happen again!" If we've been blaming ourselves and feeling like we deserved to be hurt, anger can be a wonderful relief. It can be an important tool in the healing process.

After it's done its job, though, the anger can become more of a burden than the hurt that inspired it. Sometimes we hold on to anger too long. We become obsessed with how wrong the other person was and how right we are to feel hurt and angry. We feel the hurt over and over again. That's what the word "resentment" means—feeling the feelings over and over again.

When we get stuck in anger, the anger controls us. We give up our freedom. We think we're doing it to punish those who hurt us, but *we're* being punished.

When we hold on to resentment we become angry, not only with the person who hurt us, but also with everyone who reminds us of that person, or with everyone around us. For example, a man who's been hurt by women might become angry at all women. Or a woman who's been raped might become angry at all men. In resentment, we sometimes feel angry with everyone around us. The anger becomes a large part of the way we see and define ourselves. The anger is a big factor in many of our decisions. In a very important way, the anger controls us. As it's often said, the people who hurt us are "living rent-free in our heads." Many of us have been trained to believe that if we keep feeling hurt and angry, that will somehow "punish" the people who hurt us. The sad truth is that the people who hurt us have probably decided that their own actions were justified. The only person who's being punished is the person who's obsessed with the anger, and the many people who happen to be nearby and get caught in all those angry feelings.

Letting Go of Anger

- Doesn't mean we're saying it was okay to hurt us
- Doesn't mean we'd let them do it again
- Doesn't mean we won't press charges if it was illegal
- Means we can free ourselves from the cage of our anger
- Means we move on and let the rest of the healing take place

---

Letting go of anger doesn't mean we're saying it was okay for people to hurt us. It doesn't have anything to do with the people who hurt us. Letting go doesn't mean we'd let them—or anyone else—do it again. It doesn't mean we won't press charges if what they did was illegal. It just means we can free ourselves from the cage that our anger has built around us. We can move on and let the rest of the healing process take place.[3]

Acceptance

Many people who explain the grieving process speak of acceptance as the last "stage" of grief. That's because it can be a door through the pain and into a new life. Like letting go of anger, acceptance doesn't mean we're going to put up with anything and everything that anybody might want to do to us. It doesn't mean that what happened was right, or even okay with us. It just means we accept reality for what it is, and get on with our lives.

We have many choices in the present—and these choices will affect the future—but we have no choice at all about the past. There are also a lot of things about ourselves we can't change, no matter how many things we can learn to do differently. And when it comes to other people, we can't change a thing. They might or might not choose to change, but we can't make those decisions for them or make the changes happen.

When we accept that what happened is what happened, we find new sources of strength and wisdom. We can reconnect with others and risk being close.

Acceptance is a tricky job because it means learning to tell the difference between what we can and can't change, and what we should and shouldn't try to change. Sometimes acceptance means doing nothing and simply letting things happen. Other times, it means sticking up for a principle that we believe is right. Often it means accepting the challenge of changing the way we think and act. As you can see, acceptance takes a lot of courage.

For many people, acceptance is more a spiritual decision than anything else. We get tired of fighting reality. We reach the limits of our ability to put up with denial, self-blame, anger, isolation, and depression. When we give up that fight, we find new sources of strength that are beyond anything we've experienced before. As we learn acceptance, we become new people.[4]

When we reach acceptance, we can reconnect with others. We now have the courage to risk being close to people again. We also have the wisdom that will make us more likely to find real intimacy.

Broken Dreams, Transformation, and Hope

In going through times of grieving, it's important to respect the pain and seriousness of our losses. But it's also important to remember that the grieving and healing process can lead to transformation and new hope.

Psychologist Ken Moses writes about the ways we "attach" to people, values, ideals, and even images of ourselves. We connect with them through what he calls "attachment dreams"— our hopes, wishes, and thoughts of the future. When we suffer loss, our dreams for that person or situation are shattered. After sexual violence, we might feel the loss of our beliefs about ourselves or our dreams of safety or innocence.

Ken Moses describes grieving as a process that first calls us to let go of those shattered dreams. We can't return to life as it was, because life has changed. Then we "wander dreamless" for a while, until we can build new dreams based on our new reality. During that time of wandering we question and reform the meanings and values in our lives. If we refuse to go through the feelings of grief—the anger, depression, guilt, and fear—we aren't able to do the deep work that leads toward transformation.

Transformation is much more than just changing behavior. It's an experience that changes the most important things about us: what we believe, what we think, how we feel, what we do. If we really work through our grieving and healing processes—instead of running away from them—they can lead to real transformation. Only if we have the courage to let go of the old, broken dreams can we work toward building new ones.

At the end of a transformation experience is new hope. We often find that our lives are better than they were before—sometimes even better than they were before we were hurt. We know ourselves better. We realize we've grown in ways we couldn't have predicted. We often feel closer to our sources of spiritual strength. We're rebuilding our lives with more strength, more dignity, and greater purpose than we've ever had.[5]

Notes

1. The Bibliography contains several books on rape and childhood abuse—and on recovery from those experiences—that might be useful in challenging self-blame.
2. The Bibliography lists materials on clinical depression. It also lists materials that look at depression as part of larger growth and healing processes. Examples might be M. Scott Peck's *The Road Less Traveled*, Thomas Moore's *Care of the Soul*, or Hugh Prather's *Notes on How to Live in the World and Still Be Happy*.
3. Many books in the Bibliography address issues of anger, individually and as part of a larger healing process. Three that focus specifically on anger are Carol Tavris's Anger: The Misunderstood Emotion, H. G. Lerner's *The Dance of Anger*, and *Facing the Fire* by John Lee and Bill Scott.
4. Many of the books in the Bibliography—particularly those with a Twelve-Step orientation—talk about acceptance as a tool in healing and spiritual growth. Just a few examples would be Terence T. Gorski's *Keeping the Balance*, Gerald Jampolsky's *Love Is Letting Go of Fear*, M. Scott Peck's *The Road Less Traveled*, Ernest Kurtz and Katherine Ketcham's *The Spirituality of Imperfection*, Marianne Williamson's *A Return to Love*, Thomas Moore's *Care of the Soul*, and *Tao, the Watercourse Way* by Alan Watts.
5. The Bibliography contains one article by Ken Moses, "Grief Groups: Rekindling Hope." More information on his work is available from Resource Networks, Inc., in Evanston, Illinois.

Journal Questions

1. Most people need healing from something. What areas of your life are most in need of healing? Where do you think the healing comes from?

2. How do you feel about getting help from other people? Does it feel like a practical thing to do, or does it feel weak or shameful?

3. Have you ever gotten stuck in a particular feeling of grieving? What was—or is—it like? What are some steps you might take to get "un-stuck"?

4. What experiences have you had with losing hope and finding new hope?

5. What do you need to do to heal? What will it take to heal the past and build a new future?

CHAPTER 13

Chemical Dependency, Recovery, and Sexual Aggression

Sexual force and manipulation often go hand-in-hand with another serious problem: abuse of, and addiction to, alcohol and other drugs. Each of these problems adds to—and feeds off—the other.

This chapter looks at:

- How alcohol and drugs raise the risk of sexual force and manipulation
- How these substances are used to dull the pain of sexual abuse
- The possibility of recovery from chemical dependency
- How some people try to escape the work of recovery in relationships
- The "13th step"—the danger of sex for newly recovering people
- What happens when people wait for sober relationships

Part of the link between substance abuse and sexual aggression is clear to anyone who's ever studied the subject: Men who are drinking or using other drugs are much more likely to rape or manipulate women. And women who are using those substances have much less chance of knowing and protecting their sexual limits.

It's more complicated than that, though. The effects of rape and sexual manipulation—in childhood or adult life—also raise the risk of substance abuse and addiction. This can happen whether or not there are other symptoms of PTSD. This increases their vulnerability to more victimization. It's a painful—but very common—downward spiral.

Men who were abused as children are also more likely to channel their anger and pain into substance abuse. For some people these substances lower their ability to control their actions—and unleash stored up anger and rage. After people have committed sexual violence or manipulation, they can use alcohol and other drugs to deaden their feelings of shame and guilt over what they've done. They can also use the fact that they were drunk or high to justify what happened and avoid taking responsibility for what they've done.

Many people believe that men and women who recover from chemical dependency will automatically stop having problems with sexual violence. They often don't, though. For people who are chemically dependent, recovery is the most important thing they can do to save their lives, careers, relationships, and their dignity. But some men in recovery still can't control their aggression toward women. And many women in recovery are still victimized by men—even men they meet in their recovery programs. This pattern is a common cause of relapse.

Medicating the Pain—Causing More Pain

Because substance abuse is a common reaction to the effects of trauma, people who were abused or exposed to violence as children are more likely to drink too much or use other drugs as teens and adults. What they really need is help for their emotional troubles, but they settle for an escape from the pain. Many people don't know about the counseling services available in their communities. Many others don't have access to services, don't feel as if they deserve help, or don't believe anyone can help them.

As addiction progresses, powerlessness raises the risk of sexual aggression. Aggressors might fight to regain their power. Victims might deny any choice.

This can be particularly true for women who grew up with abuse and other family problems and learned to feel helpless and hopeless early in life. Alcohol and other drugs might seem like the best way to kill the painful memories and feelings.

For both men and women, having grown up with a chemically dependent family member can make substance abuse more likely. After all, what's the most common way they've seen people deal with pain? Unfortunately, their family history also raises their genetic risk of becoming chemically dependent themselves. And their denial skills—which they learned in order to deal with childhood pain—are now used to deny their own alcohol or other drug problems.

It's not just chemical abuse that makes some people more aggressive and makes others less likely to take care of themselves. The effects of addiction itself can do that, too. For example, in chemical dependency people's denial becomes stronger and stronger with time. This can help men talk themselves into being aggressive with women and help women ignore the danger signs.

As people live with addiction, they also lose control over many areas of life, including their alcohol or other drug use.

Men who tend to be aggressive toward women might react to this loss of control by becoming more controlling and more aggressive. Women who feel hopeless and helpless in their lives and relationships might take this added loss of control as proof that there's nothing they can do to protect themselves—or as proof that they're not worth protecting.

Powerlessness vs. Helplessness

It's that very loss of control—and its feelings of powerlessness—that force many people to accept help for chemical dependency. Even though they've tried everything they know to control their use of alcohol and other drugs, it hasn't worked. They find life getting more and more crazy. They finally realize that the moment they pick up any mood-altering substance, they're powerless over it.

In treatment or recovery meetings people learn they have two choices. On one side, they have the pain and destruction that are sure to follow continued use of alcohol or other drugs. On the other side they have the benefits of a clean and sober recovery.

For those who choose it, recovery is a way to get access to better skills and real strength. People join strong support networks and learn to live healthy lives. Many people choose recovery programs that emphasize spiritual help, like Twelve-Step programs such as AA, NA, and CA. In those groups many people use their own ideas and feelings of spirituality—whatever they might be—to tap into social and spiritual power that can help them do what they couldn't do alone. There are also programs that don't focus on spiritual concepts, programs like Women for Sobriety or Rational Recovery.[1]

In recovery many people still have urges to try to control others. But they learn that those tactics didn't make them happy—and often made life a lot worse. Many people who were used to feeling like helpless victims learn they have choices and responsibilities. They also have the help they need to build fulfilling lives.

For a few people all their self-destructive life patterns begin to fade away as they come out of the chemical fog. For many, however, it's much harder than that. It takes a lot of work. And some people try to live in sobriety the same way they were living while they were drunk or high—just without the booze or drugs. It doesn't work, though. It causes more pain and often leads to relapse. As the old saying goes, "If nothing changes, nothing changes."

The Urge to Escape

When people are used to escaping pain through alcohol or other drugs, it's hard to get used to a drug-free life. Even after they clean the drugs out of their system during the first few days, the brain might take a few months—or much longer—to heal. It's usually been soaking up poison for years, and it's worked hard to adapt. Now it has to adapt to drug-free reality. This process is called "post-acute withdrawal." These changes in the brain can cause anxiety, depression, sadness, and jittery nerves for anywhere from a month to two years.

Stress in Early Sobriety

- Anxiety, depression, and sadness from left-over poison in the brain
- Nightmares and flashbacks for survivors of childhood abuse
- The pain of losses that were never really grieved
- The pain of many ordinary human emotions
- The discomfort of joy when we're used to feeling pain and anxiety

---

For people whose chemical use covered up painful memories and symptoms of PTSD, these memories and symptoms can start to return after the drugs are taken away. Survivors of childhood abuse—particularly sexual abuse—can start to have nightmares and "flashbacks" that they don't understand. They begin to have terrifying memories of events they'd forgotten completely. When that starts to happen, people need professional help to cope with those symptoms while they give their recovery time to stabilize. Then they'll need ongoing support to resolve the trauma.

Some well-meaning friends might tell them it's better not to deal with "childhood issues" for the first year of sobriety. And that's often true if the memories and feelings connected with childhood issues are successfully buried. Then they don't interfere with recovery. But for people whose feelings and memories are returning, simply trying to push them away doesn't work, and it often leads to feelings of failure. It's important to get help as soon as the memories start to surface.

Added to all this is the fact that people in early recovery are actually feeling their true feelings for the first time in years. They may have had a lot of losses that they never really grieved. And a number of everyday human feelings can be quite painful. The temptation to escape them is normal. Even feelings like joy and contentment can be scary for people who've been used to living in depression and crisis. If they have low feelings of self-worth and don't believe they deserve good things, people can be tempted to escape happy emotions too.

Escaping into Relationships

Of course, if people in recovery want to keep their sobriety, they know that alcohol and other drugs are no longer options for them. Escape into sexual relationships—the thrill of infatuation, the distraction of desire—can be a strong temptation. It's common for people in early recovery to find themselves feeling more compulsive in many areas of life, including relationships.

The trouble is that jumping from one compulsion to another isn't really recovering. It's just shifting the addictive behavior from side to side. It not only distracts people from their pain but also distracts them from the hard work of recovery. Sexual and romantic relationships—even healthy ones—are stressful even at the most stable points in people's lives. In early recovery these relationships can cause a lot of confusion and pain. They often lead to relapse.

People who were in relationships before they got sober usually face some challenges if they decide to stay involved with their partners. If their partners still drink or use, that can cause a lot of conflict. Often people who are trying to stay sober will find it very tempting—or annoying—to spend time with a partner who's drinking or using. Sometimes the partner will resent the fact that the recovering person doesn't use anymore.

> **Escape into sexual relationships—the thrill of infatuation, the distraction of desire—can be a strong temptation.**

Even partners who aren't chemically dependent often resent the time the recovering person spends at meetings, the new friends, and the healthy changes in his or her life. This can put a strain on the relationship, and the relationship can put a strain on recovery. The most important thing to remember is that recovery comes first.

The "Thirteenth Step"

An important part of the "folk wisdom" in 12-Step groups is the idea that people should avoid sexual or romantic relationships for the first year of recovery. Newcomers are often warned about the "Thirteenth Step." That's what they call it when a program member gets sexually or romantically involved with another member who's in his or her first year of sobriety.

Thirteenth stepping is a major cause of relapse, especially among women. If there's manipulation or aggression, the risk of relapse is even higher.

No matter what the circumstances are—if the newcomer seduces the older member, if they're in love, if they only "do it" once—thirteenth stepping is thought of as sexually "predatory" behavior. Whether or not the older member means to hurt the newcomer, he or she is using the newcomer in a dangerous way. That's because people are always emotionally vulnerable in early sobriety, whether they know it or not. They're much more likely to relapse. This extra vulnerability often lasts longer than the first year, particularly for women who've been victimized in the past.

Thirteenth stepping—and sexual relationships in general—are important factors in relapse. This is especially true for women in early recovery. When sex is the result of a man's manipulation or aggression, the risk of relapse is even higher. How can a woman build up her feelings of self-worth, self-confidence, and self-respect when she's being forced or pressured into having sex?

Gail is a thirty-two-year-old woman with a history of physical and sexual abuse in childhood. She's been in and out of Alcoholics Anonymous for nine years. She's gotten sober many times, and relapsed many times. And each time she relapses, it's always after she's been in a relationship for a while and stopped going to meetings. Sometimes it's someone from her past who's come back to re-connect with her. Other times it's someone she's met at her meetings.

Gail has a very low opinion of herself and feels desperately lonely. At first it always feels as if the man will take away her loneliness. But after a few months she starts feeling even worse about herself. After feeling depressed and "crazy" for a while, she finally gives in to the pressure and buys a bottle. She sees her pattern clearly, but she can't seem to stop setting the chain of events in motion. She feels as if she has no choice but to get involved with these men.

If men have used sexual force or manipulation on women in the past, they might tell themselves those tendencies disappeared as soon as they stopped drinking or using. But alcohol and other drugs don't *make* people do aggressive or abusive things. They might loosen people up and make them more angry, but they don't change people's basic urges.

There's an old saying: "If you sober up a horse thief, you get a sober horse thief." A man who manipulated or raped women before recovery is likely to do it sober, too, unless he gets help for that problem. Help is available, though, even within the 12-Step model. There are groups and other forms of therapy for people with addictive sexual histories.[2]

Many men in recovery do find themselves developing new respect for women. Gary knew that something inside him had changed the night he met Celene at an AA dance and drove her home. He had about five years' recovery at the time. Celene was a tall, beautiful blonde who had once been a professional dancer. He'd been strongly attracted to her all evening. His head was full of thoughts of what they would do when they got to her place. She asked him inside.

Then when they went into her kitchen and sat down with some coffee, Celene started talking about the program. She said she had six months' sobriety. She was starting to feel as if she was being changed by the spirituality she'd been reading about and hearing people talk about in meetings. She couldn't explain it, but she was starting to feel more peaceful. "I started seeing her as a little sister," said Gary. "All my plans for the night went out the window, and I knew I wouldn't be able to go to bed with her. I knew I was just there to help her. I talked for a while, finished my coffee, and went home."

Thirteenth Stepping by Helping Professionals

One sad fact is that some women are seduced by professionals in the chemical dependency field. These might be inpatient or outpatient counselors in their treatment centers. Sometimes people who don't have a lot of time in recovery become counselors, working for low wages without enough support and guidance from their employers.[3]

If a helping professional gets involved sexually with a client—even if the client wants to get involved—it's one of the most serious forms of betrayal. A counseling relationship is a delicate thing. The stress of sexual involvement makes that relationship very destructive for the client. The nature of the helper's role gives him or her psychological power over the client. Involvement with a counselor—or any other employee of a treatment service provider—can easily lead to relapse or to other serious emotional problems.

If you've been invited into sexual contact by a professional who's supposed to be there to help you, please don't get involved. Ask for another counselor immediately. That person is breaking strong ethical codes and shouldn't be encouraged to relate to clients in that way. He or she can't keep you safe, but you can—by finding someone else who can help you without putting you in danger.

Safety from the Thirteenth Step

Women in recovery programs need to be aware that some of the men in their programs are still likely to try to use or abuse them sexually. There will be some men they'll get to know over time and trust as friends. But until then, they need to be just as careful with "program" men as they needed to be with the men they used to meet in bars. That often means not being alone with them—in their cars, in their apartments, or wherever. It's not fair and it's not right that women should have to take these safety measures in recovery programs. But rape and manipulation are even less fair and right, and relapse can be fatal.

Women in recovery need to be just as careful with "program" men as they needed to be with the men they used to meet in bars.

In most 12-Step meetings there's some social pressure on men not to "go after" women who are new to recovery or vulnerable for other reasons. Women can use this pressure to stop men from asking them out on dates or inviting them to social activities. A woman might start by telling the man that she's still in her first year of sobriety and that she doesn't date. She can also practice her assertiveness skills on him by repeating the same sentence or saying it in a stronger way. If he still tries to ask her out or act in a sexual way, she can talk to someone she trusts who has a lot of time on the program. That person can advise her, or talk to the man about his behavior.

In one city, a group of young women age fifteen to nineteen has come up with a solution to the thirteenth-step problem.

They often attend groups with a lot of young people, and some of them have been "burned" by getting manipulated or involved too soon. When a newly sober young woman enters their meetings, they all cluster around her—almost as if they're building a nest around her. They offer her their support, give her the appropriate warnings, and let the men in the group know that it's not okay to ask her out this early in her recovery.

Some women in early sobriety are more comfortable at all-women's meetings. If there aren't enough women's meetings, though, they can also get to know other women at mixed-gender meetings. They can sit together for mutual support and travel to and from the meetings together. With time and practice, the newcomer can learn to be more assertive. She can learn that she has a right to get sober without being harassed. It's important for a woman's sobriety—and for life in general—that she learn to protect that right.

Some women would rather be in a recovery program that's just for women, like Women for Sobriety (WFS). WFS presents recovery principles in language that's tailored to women. Women should look into all the recovery choices available in their communities. But those who are suited to 12-Step programs and principles don't have to be forced out of those programs by the actions of a few men. People have a right to choose the recovery paths that best fit their needs.

Waiting for Sober Relationships

Many people decide to give their recovery a long time to stabilize before they try sex and relationships again. This gives them a chance to get to know the opposite sex as people. Once they've made a serious decision not to get involved with anyone for a while, they stop thinking of men or women as commodities. They can start to operate in the new model of relationship, even if they were used to operating in the old model.

Many people start to focus on the fact that they're all in the same program and they care about one another's sobriety. That doesn't mean they stop being attracted or even stop getting crushes. But they stop thinking only about what they want and start thinking about what they can do that will help both people.

> **Personal growth is important for everyone, but especially for people who are trying to stay clean and sober. Their lives depend on it.**

After a while recovering people begin to understand the self-destructive patterns they used to follow. People who once looked dangerously attractive just start to look dangerous. And people they used to overlook start to show some impressive signs of strength. They see healthy couples and wonder how they get along so peacefully. They start to wonder if they could get used to a peaceful relationship, too. Then they begin to understand how much work they'll have to do on themselves before they can meet that challenge.

The slow relationship-building process described in the next chapter is absolutely important for people in recovery. Personal growth is important for everyone, but especially for people who are trying to stay clean and sober. Their lives depend on it.

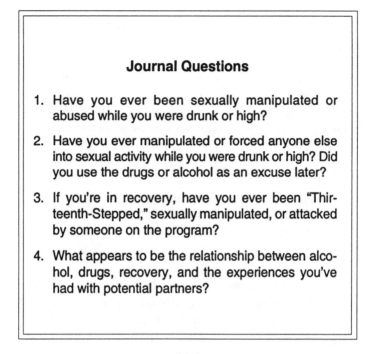

Journal Questions

1. Have you ever been sexually manipulated or abused while you were drunk or high?

2. Have you ever manipulated or forced anyone else into sexual activity while you were drunk or high? Did you use the drugs or alcohol as an excuse later?

3. If you're in recovery, have you ever been "Thirteenth-Stepped," sexually manipulated, or attacked by someone on the program?

4. What appears to be the relationship between alcohol, drugs, recovery, and the experiences you've had with potential partners?

Notes

1. If you think you might have a problem with alcohol or other drugs, it's important to get more information and the help of others who have had the same kind of problem. You can get the phone numbers of many local chapters of recovery groups—including Alcoholics Anonymous, Narcotics Anonymous, Cocaine Anonymous, and Rational Recovery—through your local telephone directory and directory assistance. Women for Sobriety has a national toll-free number (1-800-333-1606). If you can't find local numbers, three national centers keep current lists of self-help groups throughout the country. They are the Self-Help Center in Evanston, Illinois (708/328-0470); the Self-Help Clearinghouse in Denville, New Jersey (201/625-9565); and the National Self-Help Clearinghouse in New York (212/354-8525). Most recovery groups also have national headquarters, including AA (212/870-3400), NA (818/780-3951), and CA (310/559-5833).

Many people need professional help during the detoxification process and during the early weeks or months of recovery. For more information you can contact treatment centers in your community or call local or state social service agencies for referral. The National Institute on Drug Abuse (NIDA) has a treatment hotline that can provide information and referrals. To speak to someone in English, call 1-800-662-4357; and in Spanish, call 1-800-662-9832.

If you're being affected by someone else's addiction to alcohol or other drugs, you can get help from recovery groups for family members, friends, and others affected by addiction. Most of these groups have local numbers listed in telephone directories or directory assistance. Many also have national headquarters, including Al-Anon and Alateen (1-800-356-9996), Nar-Anon (310/547-5800), and Cocanon (310/859-2206).

2. Local treatment centers, community mental health centers, and private therapists can offer referral to groups and therapists who specialize in sexual addiction. The Bibliography also lists several books that address addictive sexual patterns, including *Love and Addiction* by Stanton Peele and Archie Brodsky; *Out of the Shadows* and *Don't Call It Love* by Patrick Carnes; and *Sex and Love Addicts Anonymous,* published by the Augustine Fellowship.

    There are also many mutual-help groups for people whose sexual relationships have followed addictive patterns. Local information may be available through directory assistance, or through one of the national self-help clearinghouses at 708/328-0470, 201/625-9565, or 212/354-8525. Or you can contact the national headquarters of Sex and Love Addicts Anonymous (617/332-1845), Sex Addicts Anonymous (713/869-4902), or Sexaholics Anonymous (805/581-3343).

3. Treatment professionals who want to study this question further can find more information in William White's books: *Incest in the Organizational Family, The Culture of Addiction/The Culture of Recovery,* and *Critical Incidents;* or his monograph entitled *A Systems Perspective on Sexual Exploitation of Clients by Professional Helpers.*

CHAPTER 14

Safety and Friendship

Here are two pictures:

It's morning. A young woman is walking in the sun. She's smiling to herself, thinking about something funny that her date said the night before. A year ago she'd still be in bed, probably hung over, resenting the fact that a stranger was lying next to her. But last night as she said good night and closed the door, she felt a sense of joy and freedom. She made her limits clear, and he didn't try any tricks to get inside. He didn't make her feel guilty or try to force the door. It was clear that he was attracted and so was she. But he didn't act like he needed payment for spending time with her. It was as if her company was enough for him. It was as if they were friends.

A young man is in his yard, building something. He stops to wipe his forehead and thinks about her for a minute. They had a lot of fun last night. In the old days he would have felt like a failure because he didn't score. In the old days, he might have scored no matter what it took. The things he used to do! He thought that was what it took to be a man. He never thought about what he was giving up to get sex, or how desperate he felt. Last night as he walked away from her door, he felt something strange and satisfying. It was his dignity, probably. His self-respect. It was the knowledge that he didn't have to use or abuse another human being to get what he wanted. He was free.

Going Slowly

Safety isn't boring. Friendship isn't the absence of desire. Building a relationship slowly doesn't put out the fire. It makes it last longer.

Staying safe in a new relationship doesn't depend on being and acting suspicious. In healthy relationships, people don't take things slowly just because they're afraid of sexual force and manipulation. They take things slowly because they know that gives them the best chance of having a good relationship.

More Reasons for Going Slowly

- Brain chemicals are misleading in the first few months of "love."
- We start to see people as commodities instead of friends.
- When reality sets in, we're shocked at our partner's flaws.
- We start to try to change our partner to meet our desires.
- Unless we're friends first, the relationship won't survive.

In the first few months of a sexual and/or romantic relationship, the human brain becomes a strange place. It puts out high doses of certain chemicals. These chemicals make desire and pleasure more intense, and they make the other person's most obnoxious habits look cute and cuddly. Actually, the way we look at the partner during this infatuation stage is probably the way we should look at people in general all the time: with understanding and affection.

Unfortunately, this is also the stage where commodity thinking steps in. "This feels **so** good! I want more, and I want it now!" or "This must be 'the one'! How can I *get* this person?" While the brain chemicals are still floating around and it still feels good, the commodity thinking sets up house-keeping.

Then one day: Blammo! The chemicals go away and reality sets in. Suddenly this person has *flaws*! But commodity thinking can't stand reality. It wants this person to be perfect, because he or she exists to fulfill our needs.

So we start tinkering, just a little bit, to try to get the other person to change. The trouble is, they're doing the same thing to us. So both of us dig in our heels, afraid of being the only one to change. With one hand we're holding on tight to our most obnoxious habits, and with the other hand we're pointing the finger at our partner.

Without a solid foundation in friendship, most relationships don't survive this stage. Without strong skills in respect, friendship, self-worth, self-confidence, boundaries, and communication, we end up doing and saying things we deeply regret.

The Stages and Levels of Relationship

When infatuation has our brains under chemical siege, we tend to think that what we're feeling is love. It's such a powerful emotion. Saying that it's "just" infatuation is like saying it's "just" malaria. Infatuation is a powerful force, but it's not love. Love comes much later. It comes when the chemicals are gone and the masks are down, after people decide to give up the illusion of perfection.

Romantic relationships progress through five stages. First comes the acquaintance stage—surface interaction that has little or no meaning for either person. Then comes companionship—where people's main purpose for being together is to share activities. The next stage is friendship—where people's main purpose for being together is to share one another's company and provide mutual support. Only then comes romantic love—friendship combined with sexual and sensual pleasure and satisfaction. Finally we have a committed relationship—where people make commitments to stay together and to help meet one another's social and emotional needs in the world.[1]

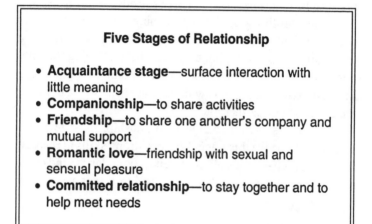

Five Stages of Relationship

- **Acquaintance stage**—surface interaction with little meaning
- **Companionship**—to share activities
- **Friendship**—to share one another's company and mutual support
- **Romantic love**—friendship with sexual and sensual pleasure
- **Committed relationship**—to stay together and to help meet needs

It's possible—and important—to try to think of *all* people in a spirit of friendship. But real friendship between two people takes time to build, even in the new model of relationship. It takes time to share experiences, earn and build trust, discover the things we have in common, and accept the ways we're different.

If we're having sex with someone and we're not true friends, then it's not romantic love. It might be companionship, or it might be a surface acquaintanceship. Calling it romantic love can set one or both of us up for disappointment.

It takes time to understand what level of sexual relationship both people want with one another. There are casual encounters, where we have sex for the purpose of enjoying sensual and sexual pleasure. There are transitional relationships, where we learn to heal and rejoin the world after the breakup of long-term relationships. And there are committed relationships.[2]

Maybe we both want committed relationships in our lives. But that doesn't mean that a committed relationship will happen between us. One person might still be healing from another relationship, and the time may not be right. Or we might not feel the same way about one another. We don't know. We won't know until we've taken the time to get to know one another.

Levels of Sexual Relationship

- **Casual encounters**—for short-term pleasure
- **Transitional relationships**—for healing after long-term relationships
- **Committed relationships**—where both people want commitment with one another at this time

---

If two people don't want the same level of relationship, getting further involved will probably bring pain to one and feelings of guilt to the other. When we're relating as friends, though, we can be honest about those things. We can put aside what we want at the moment and make decisions that support the well-being of both people.

Friendship

You might remember M. Scott Peck's definition of love, quoted in chapter four of this book: "The will to extend one's self for the purpose of nurturing one's own or another's spiritual growth."[3] Real love isn't something that comes swooping down on you and plucks you out of your life. Many have said it: Love is a decision. You make it over and over again—even with the same person.

> **True friendship is the decision to lift others up, knowing that's how we'll be lifted up.**

The same could be said of friendship, because it's really the same thing. It's a decision. It might be the decision to smile at the person behind the ticket window, for no reason except that he or she is human. It might be the decision to look at a potential partner as a human being first and put aside what we think we want from him or her. It might be the decision to set clear limits—and to respect those limits—knowing that each person's dignity is at stake.

It's the decision not to look for power in someone else's defeat. It's the decision to lift others up, that that's how we'll be lifted up. It's the knowledge that all real power is shared power. It's a willingness to rely completely on our spiritual sources of strength.

It's a slow, steady, upward journey. And it's not the end but the journey itself that sets us free.

Notes

1. For more information about the stages of relationship, see Terence T. Gorski's *Getting Love Right*.
2. For more information about levels of relationship, see Terence T. Gorski's *Getting Love Right*.
3. From *The Road Less Traveled* by M. Scott Peck.

Journal Questions

1. When you read the first two paragraphs of this chapter, how did you feel? How possible do you think this vision is?

2. Have you ever mistaken infatuation for love? How did you feel when you "crashed" from that experience?

3. Think about the people you truly consider your closest friends. What did it take to build those friendships?

4. How can you be a true friend? What can you really give to a relationship—freely, without fear, and without expectation?

Afterword to Therapists

This is a book for women and men, from their early teens through their adult years. It's designed to help people understand and avoid sexual aggression and manipulation in relationships. This includes the use of seduction, coercion, or psychological force for sexual ends. It also includes "date rape" in new or existing relationships. The book can be used alone or with the *Worth Protecting* workbook, available from Herald House/Independence Press.

These materials take a cooperative approach, affirming that men and women are not natural enemies, that both have choices and responsibilities, and that true friendship and respect is possible between the genders. Its authors are a woman and a man, each of whom has a great deal of compassion for the circumstances the opposite gender faces.

The effects of sexual force and manipulation can contribute to a number of problems that clients may experience, including problems with self-esteem; depression and anxiety among survivors of rape; substance abuse and relapse in addiction; and post-traumatic stress disorder.

New experiences of sexual force and manipulation can distract the client's energy—and the therapist's time—from the underlying work of the therapeutic process. These problems can also block clients' ability to relate to potential partners and others of the opposite gender.

The age-range for sexual force and manipulation is wide, from the increase in date rape among teens to the sexual manipulation many people encounter even in their post-menopausal years. This book has been written in simple, straightforward terms to accommodate this wide audience. However, it also reaches for a depth of understanding designed to bring about real change in belief systems, attitudes, behavior, and relationships.

Your Client

Male and female clients in a number of circumstances might find this book useful including,

- people who have a history of sexual aggression or manipulation;
- people who have been forced, coerced, or manipulated into having sex;
- women or men with a history of childhood physical, sexual, or emotional abuse;
- people in their teens or twenties, the age groups at highest risk;
- women or men returning to the dating scene after divorce or the death of their spouses;
- people who are involved in substance abuse or active chemical dependence;
- people in recovery from chemical dependence; and
- mixed- or single-gender groups looking for a discussion format that will promote personal and interpersonal growth.

Although most of the problems discussed here have more widespread effects on heterosexual relationships, many of the skills and concepts included will also be useful to gay and lesbian clients.

Worth Protecting makes it clear that survivors of rape and other forms of abuse are absolutely not to blame for the abuse they have sustained. However, it also rests on the belief that people can improve their skills at self-knowledge and self-protection, and learn to avoid or respond more effectively to potentially dangerous situations. Clients who are struggling with self-blame for having been raped might mistake that as a belief that they were negligent and somehow caused the abuse. Nothing could be further from the authors' intention.

Some clients might not be ready for this book, and its introduction into their therapy should be delayed. These include women who are newly recovering from rape or sexual manipulation, people who are in early recovery from childhood sexual abuse, and clients with cognitive problems that limit their ability to grasp abstract concepts.

What This Book Is

Worth Protecting is designed to help people understand their own social training, the training that may be affecting prospective partners, the dynamic that's created when these forces meet, and some potential consequences of that dynamic. It serves as a primer in concepts and skills related to healthy, safe development of sexual or nonsexual friendship, and in some of the skills necessary for avoiding acquaintance rape and sexual manipulation. This book focuses on the reader's individual choices and responsibilities, rather than on the rationale for blaming others.

As part of its skill-building focus, *Worth Protecting* ends each chapter with a series of journal questions. These questions can be used to stimulate thought for the client's ongoing personal journal. They also can be used in discussion groups of men, women, or mixed genders. The *Worth Protecting* workbook has exercises for individuals and groups, to help people integrate the ideas discussed in the book.

What This Book Is Not

Worth Protecting doesn't claim to serve as a therapeutic tool for recovery from rape or sexual manipulation, or from childhood abuse. It doesn't discuss any legal controversies associated with acquaintance or date rape. And it doesn't attempt to sort out the many responsibilities of individuals, institutions, and society as a whole regarding sexual force and manipulation.

The concepts and skills discussed in this book draw from, and are compatible with, a number of therapeutic disciplines, including cognitive therapy, family systems theory, child development theory, loss and grieving theory, Twelve-Step recovery principles, and relapse prevention theory.

We hope this book will enhance your clients' therapeutic process, increase their safety, and speed their progress toward healthy relationships—with others, with their healing processes, and with themselves.

Bibliography

Ackerman, Robert J. *Children of Alcoholics*, 2nd ed. New York: Simon & Schuster, 1987.

_____. *Children of Alcoholics: A Guide for Parents, Educators, and Therapists*, 2nd ed. New York: Simon & Schuster, 1983.

_____. *Growing in the Shadow*. Pompano Beach, Florida: Health Communications, 1986.

_____. *Let Go and Grow*. Pompano Beach, Florida: Health Communications, 1987.

_____. *Same House, Different Homes*. Pompano Beach, Florida: Health Communications, 1987.

Ackerman, Robert J., and Susan E. Pickering. *Abused No More: Recovery for Women from Abusive or Co-Dependent Relationships*. Bradenton, Florida: Human Services Institute, 1989.

Adams, Caren, Jennifer Fay, and Jan Loreen-Martin. *No Is Not Enough: Helping Teenagers Avoid Sexual Assault*. San Luis Obispo, California: Impact Publishers, 1984.

Alcoholics Anonymous, 3rd ed. New York: Alcoholics Anonymous World Services, 1976.

Archer, John, Ed. *Male Violence*. New York: Routledge, 1994.

Augustine Fellowship, The. *Sex and Love Addicts Anonymous*. Boston, Massachusetts: Fellowship-Wide Services, 1986.

Bader, Ellyn, and Peter T. Pearson. *In Quest of the Mythical Mate: A Developmental Approach to Diagnosis and Treatment in Couples Therapy*. New York: Brunner/Mazel, 1988.

Beattie, Melody. *Beyond Codependency, and Getting Better All the Time*. Center City, Minnesota: Hazelden, 1986.

Beattie, Melody. *Codependent No More: How to Stop Controlling Others and Start Caring for Yourself.* San Francisco: HarperSan Francisco, 1987.

Benard, Bonnie. "Resiliency Requires Changing Hearts and Minds," *Western Center News* (March 1993): 4-5.

Beneke, Timothy. *Men on Rape: What They Have to Say About Sexual Violence.* New York: St. Martin's Press, 1982.

Berkowitz, Bob, with Roger Gittines. *What Men Won't Tell but Women Need to Know.* New York: Avon Books, 1990.

Black, Claudia. *Double Duty.* New York: Ballantine Books, 1990.

_____. *It Will Never Happen to Me.* Denver, Colorado: M.A.C., 1982.

_____. *My Dad Loves Me, My Dad Has a Disease.* Denver, Colorado: M.A.C., 1979.

_____. *Repeat After Me.* Denver, Colorado: M.A.C., 1985.

Boumil, Marcia Mobilia, Joel Friedman, and Barbara Ewert Taylor. *Date Rape: The Secret Epidemic.* Deerfield Beach, Florida: Health Communications, 1993.

Bowden, Julie, and Herbert Gravitz. *Genesis: Spirituality in Recovery from Childhood Traumas.* Pompano Beach, Florida: Health Communications, 1988.

Bradshaw, John. *Bradshaw on the Family: A Revolutionary Way of Self-Discovery.* Deerfield Beach, Florida: Health Communications, 1988.

_____. *Creating Love: The Next Great Stage of Growth.* New York: Bantam, 1992.

_____. *Homecoming: Reclaiming and Championing Your Inner Child.* New York: Bantam Books, 1990.

Brown, Stephanie. *Safe Passage: Recovery for Adult Children of Alcoholics.* New York: John Wiley & Sons, 1992.

_____. *Treating Adult Children of Alcoholics: A*

Developmental Perspective. New York: John Wiley & Sons, 1988.

Campbell, Anne. *Men, Women, and Aggression.* New York: Basic Books, 1993.

Carnes, Patrick. *Out of the Shadows: Understanding Sexual Addiction.* CompCare Publications, 1992.

_____. *Don't Call It Love: Recovery From Sexual Addiction.* New York: Bantam Books, 1991.

Carter, Christine. *The Other Side of Silence.* (To be published in January 1995. For more information contact Avocus Press, 1-800-345-6665.)

Cassell, Carol. *Swept Away: Why Women Confuse Love and Sex.* New York: Simon & Schuster, 1984.

Castine, J. *Recovery from Rescuing.* Deerfield Beach, Florida: Health Communications, 1989.

Cermak, Timmen A. *A Time to Heal.* Los Angeles: Jeremy P. Tarcher, 1988.

_____. *Diagnosing and Treating Co-Dependence: A Guide for Professionals Who Work with Chemical Dependents, Their Spouses and Children.* Minneapolis, Minnesota: Johnson Institute Books, 1986.

Chesanow, Neil. "Sex, Lies, and Dating: What's Really on His Mind?" *New Woman* (August 1994): 100-130.

Clarke, J.I. *Self-Esteem: A Family Affair.* New York: Harper & Row, 1978.

Cowan, Connell, and M. Kinder. *Smart Women—Foolish Choices.* New York: Clarkson N. Potter, 1985.

Creighton, Allan, and Paul Kivel. *Helping Teens Stop Violence: A Practical Guide for Educators, Counselors, and Parents.* Alameda, California: Hunter House, 1992.

Crichton, Sarah. "Sexual Correctness: Has It Gone Too Far?" *Newsweek* (October 25, 1993): 52-58.

Curran, Dolores. *Traits of a Healthy Family.* Minneapolis, Minnesota: Winston Press, 1983.

Dowling, C. *The Cinderella Complex*. New York: Summit Books, 1981.

Ellis, D. *Growing Up Stoned*. Pompano Beach, Florida: Health Communications, 1987.

Erikson, Erik H. *Childhood and Society*, 2nd ed. New York: W.W. Norton & Company, 1963.

Flannery, Raymond B., Jr. *Post-Traumatic Stress Disorder: The Victim's Guide to Healing and Recovery*. New York: The Crossroad Publishing Company, 1992.

Forward, Susan, and Craig Buck. *Obsessive Love: When It Hurts Too Much to Let Go*. New York: Bantam Books, 1991.

Forward, Susan, and Joan Torres. *Men Who Hate Women and the Women Who Love Them*. New York: Bantam Books, 1986.

Fossum, M.A., and M.J. Mason. *Facing Shame: Families in Recovery*. New York: W.W. Norton & Co., 1986.

Friday, Nancy. *My Mother, Myself: The Daughter's Search for Identity*. New York: Dell Publishing, 1977.

Friedman, Edwin H. *Generation to Generation: Family Process in Church and Synagogue*. New York: Guilford Press, 1985.

_____. *Men Are Just Desserts*. New York: Warner Books, 1983.

Friel, John C. *The Grown-up Man: Heroes, Healing, Honor, Hurt, Hope*. Deerfield Beach, Florida: Health Communications, 1991.

Friel, John C., and Linda D. Friel. *An Adult Child's Guide to What Is "Normal."* Deerfield Beach, Florida: Health Communications, 1990.

Funk, Ross. *Stopping Rape: A Challenge for Men*. Philadelphia: Inland, 1993.

Garbarino, James, Edna Guttmann, and Janis Wilson Seeley. *The Psychologically Battered Child*. San Francisco: Jossey-Bass Publishers, 1986.

Garbarino, James, Kathleen Kostelny, and Nancy Dubrow. *No Place to Be a Child: Growing Up in a War Zone.* Lexington, Massachusetts: Lexington Books, 1991.

Gil, Eliana. *Outgrowing the Pain: A Book For and About Adults Abused as Children.* New York: Dell Publishing, 1983.

Glenn, H. Stephen, and Jane Nelson. *Raising Children for Success: Blueprints and Building Blocks for Developing Capable People.* Fair Oaks, California: Sunrise Press, 1987.

Gordon, Sol. *Why Love Is Not Enough.* Boston, Massachusetts: Bob Adams, 1988.

Gorski, Terence T. *Getting Love Right: Learning the Choices of Healthy Intimacy.* New York: Simon & Schuster, 1993.

_____. *Keeping the Balance: A Psychospiritual Model of Growth and Development.* Independence, Missouri: Herald House/Independence Press, 1993.

_____. *Understanding the Twelve Steps.* New York: Simon & Schuster, 1989.

Gottman, John, with Nan Silver. *Why Marriages Succeed or Fail: What You Can Learn from the Breakthrough Research to Make Your Marriage Last.* New York: Simon & Schuster, 1994.

Gravitz, H.D., and J. Bowden. *Guide to Recovery: A Book for Adult Children of Alcoholics.* Holmes Beach, Florida: Learning Publications, 1985.

Gravitz, H.L. *Handbook for Children of Alcoholics.* South Laguna, California: The National Association for Children of Alcoholics, 1985.

Gray, John. *Men Are From Mars, Women Are From Venus.* New York: Harper Collins, 1993.

Grubman-Black, Stephen D. *Broken Boys/Mending Men: Recovery from Childhood Sexual Abuse.* Bradenton, Florida: Human Services Institute, 1990.

Halas, C. and R. Matteson. *I've Done So Well—Why Do I Feel*

So Bad? New York: Macmillan, 1978.

Hendrix, Harville. *Getting the Love You Want.* New York: Harper Collins, 1990.

_____. *Keeping the Love You Find.* New York: Pocket Books, 1993.

_____. *The Couples Companion: Meditations and Exercises for Getting the Love You Want.* New York: Simon & Schuster, 1994.

Hooper, Judith, and Dick Teresi. *The Three-Pound Universe.* New York: Jeremy P. Tarcher/Perigree Books, 1986.

Hope and Recovery: A Twelve Step Guide for Healing from Compulsive Sexual Behavior. Minneapolis, Minnesota: CompCare Publishers, 1989.

Hunter, Mic. *Abused Boys: The Neglected Victims of Sexual Abuse.* New York: Fawcett Columbine, 1990.

Jampolsky, Gerald G. *Love Is Letting Go of Fear.* Berkeley, California: Celestial Arts, 1979.

Jeffers, Susan. *Feel the Fear and Do It Anyway.* New York: Fawcett Columbine, 1987.

Katz, Jack. *Seductions of Crime: Moral and Sensual Attractions in Doing Evil.* New York: Basic Books, 1988.

Keen, Sam. *Fire in the Belly: On Being a Man.* New York: Bantam Books, 1991.

Kirkpatrick, J. *Turnabout.* New York: Bantam Books, 1986.

Kivel, Paul. *Men's Work: How to Stop the Violence That Tears Our Lives Apart.* New York: Ballantine Books, 1992.

Kotulak, Ronald. "Unlocking the Mind: The Biology of Violence," Chicago Tribune (Series, December 12-15, 1993).

Kritzberg, W. *The Adult Children of Alcoholics Syndrome: From Discovery to Recovery.* Pompano Beach, Florida: Health Communications, 1985.

Kurtz, Ernest. *Shame and Guilt: Characteristics of the Dependency Cycle.* Center City, Minnesota: Hazelden Foundation, 1981.

Kurtz, Ernest, and Katherine Ketcham. *The Spirituality of Imperfection: Storytelling and the Journey to Wholeness.* New York: Bantam Books, 1992.

Larson, Earnie. *Stage II Relationships: Love Beyond Addiction.* New York: Harper & Row, 1987.

Ledray, Linda E. *Recovering from Rape.* New York: Henry Holt and Company, 1986.

Lee, John. *The Flying Boy: Healing the Wounded Man.* Deerfield Beach, Florida: Health Communications, 1989.

Lee, John, with Bill Scott. *Facing the Fire: Experiencing and Expressing Anger Appropriately.* New York: Bantam Books, 1993.

Leman, K. *The Pleasers: Women Who Can't Say No—and the Men Who Control Them.* New York: Dell Publishing, 1987.

Lerner, H.G. *The Dance of Anger: A Woman's Guide to Changing the Patterns of Intimate Relationships.* New York: Harper & Row, 1985.

Lewis, D., and C. Williams. *Providing Care for Children of Alcoholics.* Pompano Beach, Florida: Health Communications, 1986.

Mauro-Cochrane, Jeanette. *Self-Respect and Sexual Assault.* Blue Ridge Summit, Pennsylvania: McGraw-Hill, 1993.

McCay, Matthew, Martha Davis, and Patrick Fanning. *Messages: The Communication Skills Book.* Oakland, California: New Harbinger Publications, 1983.

McGill, Michael E. *The McGill Report on Male Intimacy.* New York: Holt, Rinehart and Winston, 1985.

McKay, Matthew, and Patrick Fanning. *Self-Esteem: A Proven Program of Cognitive Techniques for Assessing, Improving, and Maintaining Your Self-Esteem.* Oakland, California: New Harbinger Publications, 1987.

McKay, Matthew, Peter D. Rogers, and Judith McKay. *When Anger Hurts: Quieting the Storm Within.* Oakland, California: New Harbinger Publications, 1989.

Medea, Andra. *From Conflict to Respect*. (To be published in 1995. For more information contact Medea and Associates, 200 N. Michigan #401, Chicago, IL 60601.)

Medea, Andra, and Kathleen Thompson. *Against Rape*. New York: Ferrar, Straus and Giroux, 1974.

Mellody, Pia, Andrea Wells Miller, and J. Keith Miller. *Facing Codependence*. New York: Harper & Row, 1989.

Miller, Alice. *For Your Own Good: Hidden Cruelty in Child-Rearing and the Roots of Violence*. New York: The Noonday Press, 1983.

_____. *The Drama of the Gifted Child: The Search for the True Self*. New York: Basic Books, 1981.

_____. *Thou Shalt Not Be Aware: Society's Betrayal of the Child*. New York: Penguin Books, 1984.

Moore, Thomas. *Care of the Soul: A Guide for Cultivating Depth and Sacredness in Everyday Life*. New York: HarperCollins, 1992.

_____. *Soul Mates: Honoring the Mysteries of Love and Relationship*. New York: HarperCollins, 1994.

Moses, Ken. "Grief Groups: Rekindling Hope," *Voices* (Summer 1994): 70-77.

Moses, Ken, with Robert Kearney. "Shattered Dreams and Growth: Loss and the Art of Grief Counseling." Workshop, Evanston, Illinois, 1983.

Naireh, S., and G. Smith. *Why Can't Men Open Up?* New York: Warner Books, 1983.

NiCarthy, Ginny, and Sue Davidson. *You Can Be Free: An Easy-to-Read Handbook for Abused Women*. Seattle, Washington: The Seal Press, 1989.

Nichols, Michael P. *No Place to Hide: Facing Shame So We Can Find Self-Respect*. New York: Simon & Schuster, 1991.

Norwood, Chris. Advice for Life: A Woman's Guide to AIDS Risks and Prevention. New York: Pantheon Books, 1987.

Norwood, Robin. *Women Who Love Too Much*. New York:

Simon & Schuster, 1985.

Parkinson, Frank. *Post-Trauma Stress*. Tucson, Arizona: Fisher Books, 1993.

Parrot, Andrea, and Laurie Bechhofer, eds. *Acquaintance Rape: The Hidden Crime*. New York: John Wiley & Sons, 1991.

Peck, M. Scott. *People of the Lie: The Hope for Healing Human Evil*. New York: Simon and Schuster, 1983.

_____. *The Road Less Traveled*. New York: Simon & Schuster, 1978.

Peele, Stanton, and Archie Brodsky. *Love and Addiction*. New York: Signet Books, 1975.

Prather, Hugh. *Notes on How to Live in the World and Still Be Happy*. New York: Doubleday, 1986.

_____. *Notes on Love and Courage*. New York: Doubleday, 1977.

Prather, Hugh, and Gayle Prather. *A Book for Couples*. New York: Doubleday, 1988.

_____. *I Will Never Leave You: How Couples Can Achieve the Power of Lasting Love*. New York: Bantam, 1995.

Prevention Resource Center. *Breaking the Chain: Making Prevention Programs Work for Children of Addicted Families*. Springfield, Illinois: Prevention Resource Center, 1991.

_____. *Increase the Peace: A Primer on Fear, Violence and Transformation*. Springfield, Illinois: Prevention Resource Center, 1994.

Restak, Richard M. *The Mind*. New York: Bantam Books, 1988.

Roy, Maria. *Children in the Crossfire: Violence in the Home—How Does It Affect Our Children?* Deerfield Beach, Florida: Health Communications, 1988.

Rubin, Lillian B. *Intimate Strangers: Men and Women Together*. New York: Harper & Row, 1983.

Sanford, Linda T. *Strong at the Broken Places: Overcoming the Trauma of Childhood Abuse*. New York: Avon Books, 1990.

Satir, Virginia. *Peoplemaking*. Palo Alto, California: Science & Behavior Books, 1972.

Schaef, Anne Wilson. *Codependence: Misunderstood—Mistreated*. Minneapolis, Minnesota: Winston Press, 1986.

_____. *When Society Becomes an Addict*. San Francisco: Harper & Row, 1987.

Schaeffer, B. *Is It Love or Is It Addiction?* Center City, Minnesota: Hazelden, 1987.

Silverstein, Olga, and Beth Rashbaum. *The Courage to Raise Good Men*. New York: Viking, 1994.

_____. "Why Men Beat Women: We Raise Our Boys to Be 'Heroes,'" *Chicago Tribune* (July 29, 1994): 19.

Simon, Sidney B., and Suzanne Simon. *Forgiveness: How to Make Peace with Your Past and Get on with Your Life*. New York: Warner Books, 1990.

Smith, A. *Grandchildren of Alcoholics*. Pompano Beach, Florida: Health Communications, 1988.

Smolowe, Jill. "When Violence Hits Home," *Time* 144, no. 1 (July 4, 1994): 18–25.

Solomon, Robert C. *Love: Emotion, Myth and Metaphor*. Buffalo, New York: Prometheus Books, 1990.

Steinem, Gloria. *Revolution From Within: A Book of Self-Esteem*. Boston: Little, Brown and Company, 1992.

Stern, Gail. "Women Victims of Violent Crime," *CJ the Americas* 7, no. 4 (August-September 1994): 15–16.

Stoltenberg, John. *The End of Manhood: A Book for Men of Conscience*. New York: Penguin Books, 1993.

Storr, Anthony. *Human Destructiveness*. New York: Grove Weidenfeld, 1991.

Stauss, William, et al. *13th Gen: Abort, Retry, Ignore, Fail?* New York: Vintage Books, 1993.

Subby, Robert. *Lost in the Shuffle: The Co-Dependent Reality.* Pompano Beach, Florida: Health Communications, 1987.

Tannen, Deborah. *You Just Don't Understand: Women and Men in Conversation.* New York: William Morrow and Company, 1990.

Tavris, Carol. *Anger: The Misunderstood Emotion.* New York: Simon & Schuster, 1982.

_____. *The Mismeasure of Woman.* New York: Simon and Schuster, 1992.

Tiebout, Harry M. *The Ego Factors in Surrender in Alcoholism.* New Brunswick, New Jersey: Hazelden, 1954. Reprint (vol. 15, pp. 610–621).

Twelve Steps and Twelve Traditions. New York: Alcoholics Anonymous World Services, 1952.

Twerski, A.J. *Like Yourself and Others Will, Too.* New York: Prentice Hall, 1978.

Warshaw, Robin. *I Never Called It Rape: The Ms. Report on Recognizing, Fighting and Surviving Date and Acquaintance Rape.* New York: HarperPerennial, 1988.

Watts, Alan W. *Nature, Man and Woman.* New York: Pantheon Books, 1958.

Watts, Alan, with Al Chung-liang Huang. *Tao, the Watercourse Way.* New York: Pantheon Books, 1975.

Wegscheider, Sharon. *Another Chance: Hope and Health for the Alcoholic Family.* Palo Alto, California: Science and Behavior Books, 1980.

_____. *Choice-Making for Co-Dependents, Adult Children and Spirituality Seekers.* Pompano Beach, Florida: Health Communications, 1985.

Westberg, Granger E. *Good Grief.* Philadelphia: Fortress Press, 1962.

Wheelis, Allen. *How People Change.* New York: Harper & Row, 1973.

White, William L. *Critical Incidents: Ethical Issues in Sub-*

stance Abuse Prevention and Treatment. Bloomington, Illinois: Lighthouse Training Institute, 1990.

_____. *The Culture of Addiction, the Culture of Recovery*. Bloomington, Illinois: Lighthouse Institute, 1990.

_____. *A Systems Perspective on Sexual Exploitation of Clients by Professional Helpers*. Bloomington, Illinois: Lighthouse Institute, 1993.

White, William L., and Rita Chaney. *Metaphors of Transformation: Feminine and Masculine*. Bloomington, Illinois: Lighthouse Institute, 1993.

Whitfield, C. *Healing the Child Within*. Pompano Beach, Florida: Health Communications, 1987.

Wilber, Ken. *No Boundary: Eastern and Western Approaches to Personal Growth*. Boston: Shambala, 1985.

Williamson, Marianne. *A Return to Love: Reflections on the Principles of a Course in Miracles*. New York: HarperPerennial, 1993.

_____. *A Woman's Worth*. New York: Ballantine, 1993.

Wilson, R. Reid. *Don't Panic: Taking Control of Anxiety Attacks*. New York: Harper & Row, 1986.

Woititz, Janet G. *Adult Children of Alcoholics*. Pompano Beach, Florida: Health Communications, 1987.

_____. *Healing Your Sexual Self*. Deerfield Beach, Florida: Health Communications, 1989.

_____. *Struggle for Intimacy*. Pompano Beach, Florida: Health Communications, 1987.

Wolf, Naomi. *Fire with Fire: The New Female Power and How It Will Change the 21st Century*. New York: Random House, 1993.

_____. *The Beauty Myth: How Images of Beauty Are Used Against Women*. New York: William Morrow and Company, 1991.

Wolin, Steven J., and Sybil Wolin. *The Resilient Self: How*

Survivors of Troubled Families Rise Above Adversity. New York: Villard Books, 1993.

Zielke, Sigurd H., and Margaret L. Lambooy. *Kids of the 90s: Youth on the Brink of the 21st Century.* (To be published in 1995. For information contact Koala Hospitals and Counseling Centers, 1-800-562-5212.)

Zweig, Connie, and Jeremiah Abrams, eds. *Meeting the Shadow: The Hidden Power of the Dark Side of Human Nature.* Los Angeles: Jeremy P. Tarcher, 1991.

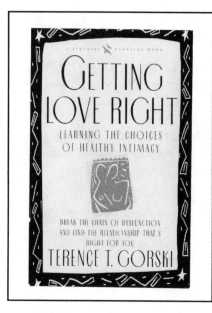

GETTING LOVE RIGHT
Learning the Choices of Healthy
Intimacy
by Terence T. Gorski
    Designed to effect change, this
book offers more than theory. It
provides the skills to develop healthy
relationships. Self-assessments and
questionnaires at the end of each
chapter help readers apply principles
and practical skills to their own lives
and move toward true, healthy
intimacy.
      52-290140 (book)

Video- and audiotape series
GETTING LOVE RIGHT
    A three-part PBS series that offers an entertaining and practical look at
healthy and dysfunctional relationships. Designed for both singles and couples.
Gorski points out that all relationships have three players--me, you, and us--and
that healthy relationships require skills that people can learn, practice, and
perfect.

TAPE 1: PERSONAL GROWTH FOR HEALTHY INTIMACY
    55-094830 (Videotape)
    55-095210 (Audiotape)

TAPE 2: PARTNER SELECTION
    55-094910 (Videotape)
    55-095480 (Audiotape)

TAPE 3: RELATIONSHIP BUILDING
    55-095050 (Videotape)
    55-095560 (Audiotape)

SETS:
    55-095130 Set of three videotapes
    55-095640 Set of three audiotapes

    To order: Call 1-800-767-8181 or (816) 252-5010
        Canadian residents 1-800-373-8382

RELATIONSHIP BUILDING AND TRANSFORMING
The Levels of Platonic and Erotic Love
by Terence T. Gorski

Gorski describes compulsive, healthy, and apathetic relationship styles and the five levels of relationship building–acquaintanceship, companionship, friendship, romantic love, and committed love. He also describes the levels of erotic relationships, including attraction, flirtation, sensual involvement, and sexual involvement.

17-022460 (Book)
17-022540 (Four audiotapes)

Videotape series:

ADDICTIVE RELATIONSHIPS
by Terence T. Gorski and
Claudia Black

TAPE 1: THE PLAYERS AND THE PERSONALITIES
This presentation defines the characteristics of addictive relationships and the traits that lock the partners together.
17-017030 (VHS)

TAPE 2: RELATIONSHIP STYLES
Relationships operate on a continuum of health ranging from compulsive to apathetic. This presentation reviews the characteristics of three relationship styles.
17-017110 (VHS)

TAPE 3: RELATIONSHIP BUILDING
Recovery is possible, and this presentation shows how it is done through the three C's–communication, caring, and commitment.
17-017380 (VHS)

SET:
17-017460 (Three-tape set)

To order: Call 1-800-767-8181 or (816) 252-5010
Canadian residents 1-800-373-8382